SUPERCHARGED SYMBOLS

MANIFESTING WITH SACRED GEOMETRY AND RUNES

IVA KENAZ

ISBN: 978-80-11-00543-6

CONTENTS

ACKNOWLEDGMENTS

I would like to thank my mom Ivana Axman for her help with this book, and especially for her wonderful artistic expertize. I also thank my husband Gunnar Tryggvason for all his loving advice and help. Moreover, big appreciation goes to my friend Hjalmar Einarsson for his brilliant insights and to my editor Jenny Papworth who provides such great support for my books.

Finally, very special thanks go to my dear friend Shelly, an amazingly gifted healer who helped me charge the symbols in this book with even more healing, shielding, and manifesting power.

With eternal love and appreciation,
I dedicate this book to Shelly.

AUTHOR'S NOTE

For almost two decades, I have been researching the magical correlations between sacred geometry, symbols, and runes. I have also been testing various methods of working with these magical shapes in healing, shielding, alchemizing, and manifesting practices.

Geometric symbols and runes have profoundly enriched my life and broadened my consciousness. They have helped me heal from past traumas, shielded me from negative energies on many occasions, bettered my psychic abilities, and ignited important spiritual realizations, to name just a few examples. Furthermore, they have helped me recognize my life's calling and attract new work opportunities, like-minded friends, and my dream home. I have also observed some incredible results with my family members and friends. It keeps amazing me how geometric symbols and runes support our inner healers, magicians, and alchemists.

After publishing my book *Sacred Geometry and Magical Symbols*, I have been continuously asked to share practical examples of how to combine individual symbols for magical workings. And so I have created the 100 supercharged symbols, which bind some of the most powerful geometries, symbols, and runes. They were carefully chosen and based on extensive research as well as practice. Additionally, they were blessed and charged with energy healing for an even stronger effect. If you are called to create your own symbols, please feel free to take mine as an inspiration. In any case, I hope that these symbols will be wonderful guides to you!

PART I

BASICS AND PRACTICAL SUGGESTIONS

THE TRADITION OF BINDING GEOMETRIES AND RUNES INTO MAGIC SYMBOLS

Binding geometries into magic symbols is a very ancient tradition. The practice has been around since the Paleolithic period and has endured into the present day. Geometric symbols have always played important roles, particularly in spirituality and magic. For many ancient cultures, geometry was considered sacred, and the term "sacred geometry" still refers to the belief that geometries have philosophical and magical attributes. This goes hand in hand with magic, as geometries are the blueprints of symbols and runes.

Perhaps the most acclaimed symbols are the Seals of Solomon, which come from Jewish and Islamic mystical traditions. They were used to channel spirits, angels, and deities but also to heal, shield, and achieve prosperity and success. Iron Age cultures carried on the tradition of binding geometric symbols and bound them with the runes: magical codes used not only for writing but also for divination, shielding, and manifesting. The Northern European tribes have preserved the legacy of the runes, but the codes themselves are far more ancient, and their predecessors can be seen in the earliest artwork known to humankind.

Though magic symbols were demonized during the Dark Ages, geometric symbols were widely used in architecture, especially in temples and cathedrals, where they were incorporated into stained-glass art, tiling, and the general décor. Geometric symbols and runes experienced a significant rise from the seventeenth to nineteenth centuries, as they were used by alchemists, occult practitioners, and members of Western esoteric schools. From then on, many magic symbols have been rediscovered and popularized. The most proclaimed Eastern symbols used to this day are the reiki symbols, which were used in ancient Japan for energy work and reintroduced to the world by Dr. Mikao Usui.

GEOMETRIES AND RUNES IN NATURE

Sacred geometry is a philosophy based around the concept that geometries are the blueprints of this world's matrix. The ancients knew well that if this reality was a manifestation of geometrical figures, then it made sense that these shapes may also help us manifest our own realities.

Most magic symbols are geometrical, and the same goes for the runes, which are concealed in countless geometries, especially the six-fold ones such as the Flower of Life, Seed of Life, hexagon, hexagram, and cube.

Words are not enough to describe the interconnections because only a visual representation can unveil them. So here are some examples of sacred geometry symbols and runes recurring in nature, from microcosm to macrocosm:

Six-pointed stars in snowflakes.

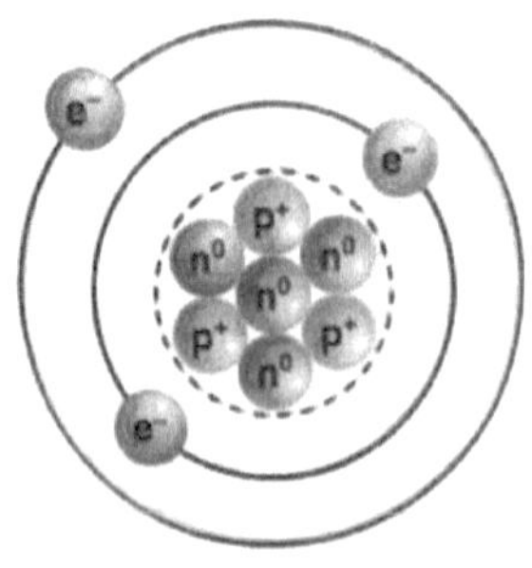

Hexagonal structure of the atom.

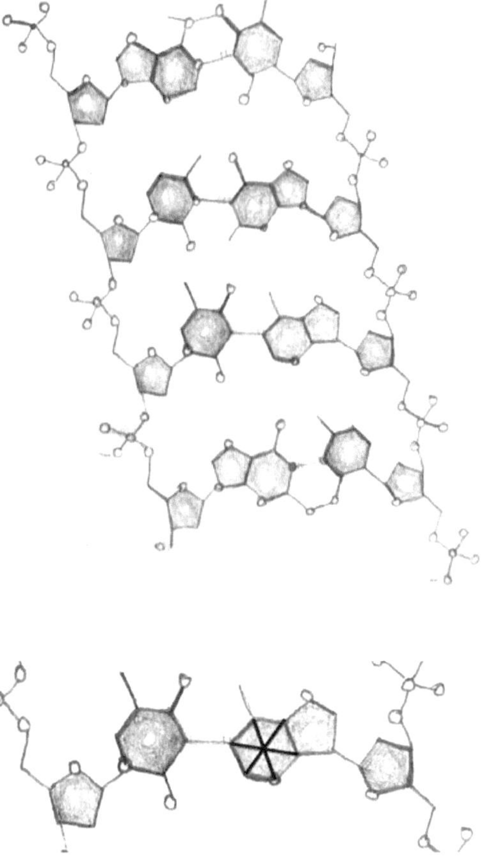

The pentagon/pentagram and hexagon/hexagram in the molecular structure of the DNA double helix.

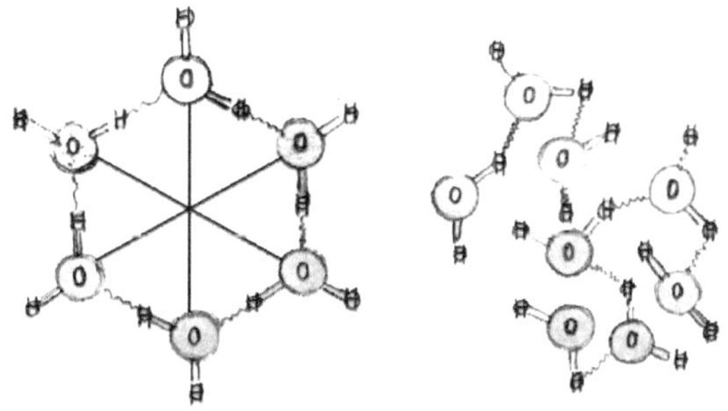

Frozen water molecules form a hexagonal pattern.

Seed of Life compared to the development of human fetus.

The path of Venus forms a pentagram around the sun every eight years.

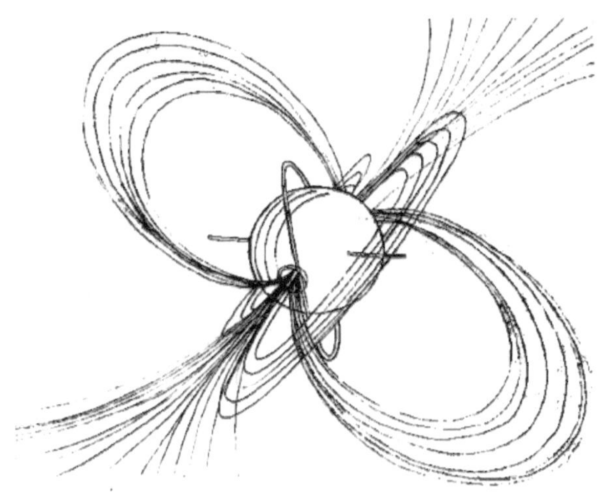

Toroidial and figure-of-eight shape of planetary electromagnetic fields.

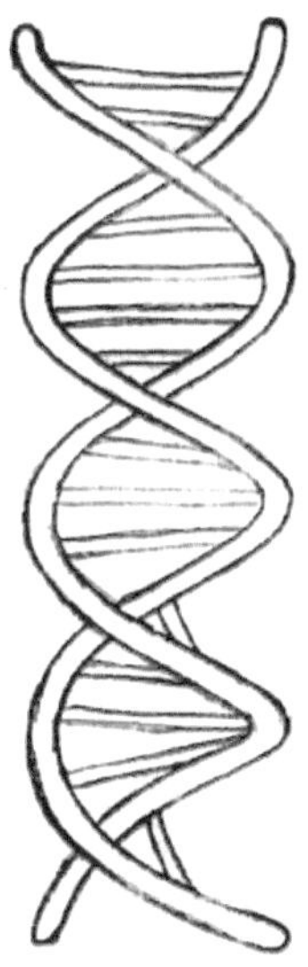

Spiral and figure-of-eight shape in DNA.

Flowers are usually pentagonal.

Pentagram in an apple core.

Clover leaves make a triangle.

Runes seen in nature.

Runes seen in nature.

GEOMETRIES AND RUNES BOUND IN THE 100 SUPERCHARGED SYMBOLS

GENERALITIES

Rounded and asymmetrical geometries and symbols bring about progress and motion. They represent the energizing part of manifestation. Straight and symmetrical symbols help us stabilize and support the grounding part of manifestation. However, there's a bit of asymmetry in symmetry and a bit of symmetry in asymmetry, so it's best to combine them.

THE CIRCLE

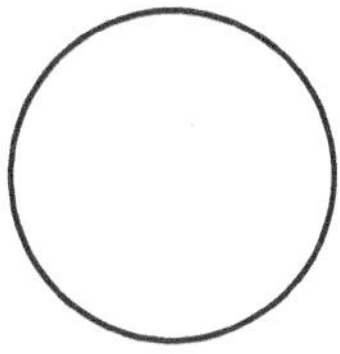

Beauty is in simplicity, and the circle is a perfect example. This simple yet profound symbol represents wholeness, completion, interconnectedness, and shielding. It's the source of all the other geometric shapes, and all the geometries find harmony in its embrace. That's why it's a symbol of perfect unity between the individual and the whole.

KEYWORDS FOR MANIFESTATION, SHIELDING, HEALING, AND OTHER PROPERTIES:

Wholeness, completion, complete harmony, shielding one's space, the all within one, the one within all.

SPIRALS

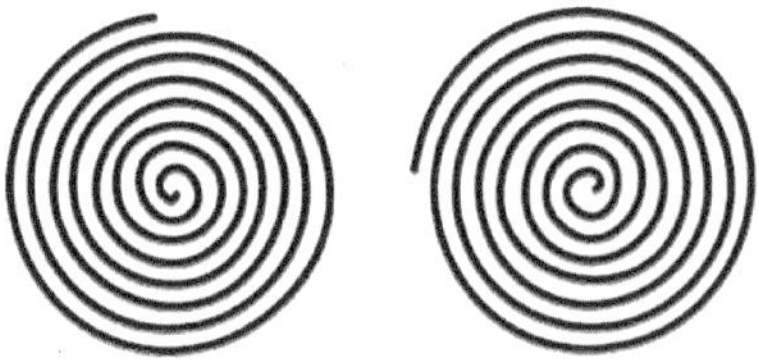

Spirals represent the circle in motion. They symbolize the energy of the life force, infinity, and healing. The left-turning spiral is connected to the past and soothing feminine energy. The right-turning spiral stands for the future and active masculine energy. A spiral naturally sets things in motion; that's why it's often used in healing.

KEYWORDS FOR MANIFESTATION, SHIELDING, HEALING, AND OTHER PROPERTIES:

Healing (the left-turning spiral heals the past and the feminine while the right-turning spiral heals the future and the masculine), energy flow, movement, progress, revitalization, rejuvenation.

Note: The superstition that the left-turning spiral has a negative effect comes from a prejudice against the feminine because the left side has always been connected to feminine energy and past events. Personally, I don't resonate with this superstition and have only had benevolent experiences of left-turning spirals.

MANDORLA AND VESICA PISCIS

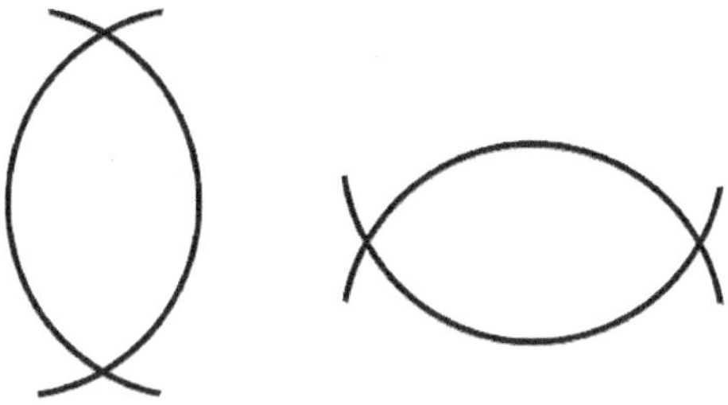

In geometry, all shapes arise from the circle and subsequently from the vesica piscis. The vesica piscis is the shape that we see in the center of two intersected circles of the same circumference. The horizontal version of the vesica piscis resembles an eye and signifies inner sight and clairvoyance. Since the Latin name translates as "fish bladder," it also relates to the water element and so to emotional healing, intuition, and psychic abilities.

The vertical version of the vesica piscis is the mandorla (an Italian word for almond), which symbolizes a gateway into the other realms as well as a new beginning. Moreover, it has been associated with the divine feminine because of its resemblance to the vulva.

KEYWORDS FOR MANIFESTATION, SHIELDING, HEALING, AND OTHER PROPERTIES:

Psychic gifts, meditation, intuition, clairvoyance, telepathy, divination, dreams, spiritual guidance, astral projection, new beginnings, emotional healing, rejuvenation, revitalization, gateways between the other realms in the World Tree of Life.

SQUARES AND CROSSES

Squares and crosses are symbols of stability and grounding. They represent the solidifying and fortifying process of manifestation. Encircled crosses or squares stand for the coalescence of the spiritual and physical dimensions, heaven and earth, body and soul, or an idea and its manifestation. Furthermore, encircled crosses sometimes signify the yearly cycles, the worldly directions, and the unity of the basic elements.

In many religions and philosophies, crosses are believed to be highly protective symbols. Equilateral crosses in particular have a wonderful shielding quality and bring about security. In some ancient cultures, crosses, six-pointed, and eight-pointed stars also represented the World Tree of Life.

KEYWORDS FOR MANIFESTATION, SHIELDING, HEALING, AND OTHER PROPERTIES:

Making things happen, security, balance, defining, stabilizing, strengthening, sustaining, centering, grounding, marking, shielding, protecting.

EIGHT-POINTED STARS AND OCTAGON

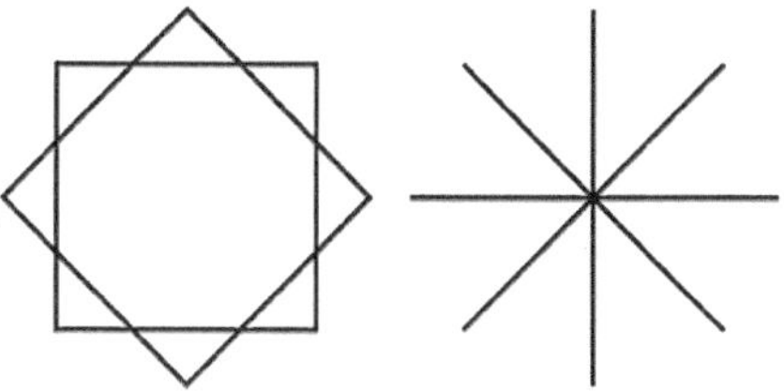

The octagon, octagram, and other eight-pointed stars accentuate the symbolism of the square and cross, which gives them double grounding, stabilizing, balancing, and shielding qualities. In some cultures, they have represented the World Tree and the unity of all its realms, therefore the multiverse. An encircled eight-pointed star signifies the pagan wheel of the year.

Throughout history, the eight-pointed star has also been known as the goddess star and signified goddesses such as the Mesopotamian Ishtar and Inanna or the Egyptian Seshat.

KEYWORDS FOR MANIFESTATION, SHIELDING, HEALING, AND OTHER PROPERTIES:

Profound grounding and stabilizing, securing, shielding, strong psychic protection, the eight pagan holidays, the cardinal and intermediate worldly directions of the compass, the World Tree, the multiverse.

UPWARD AND DOWNWARD TRIANGLES AND TETRAHEDRONS

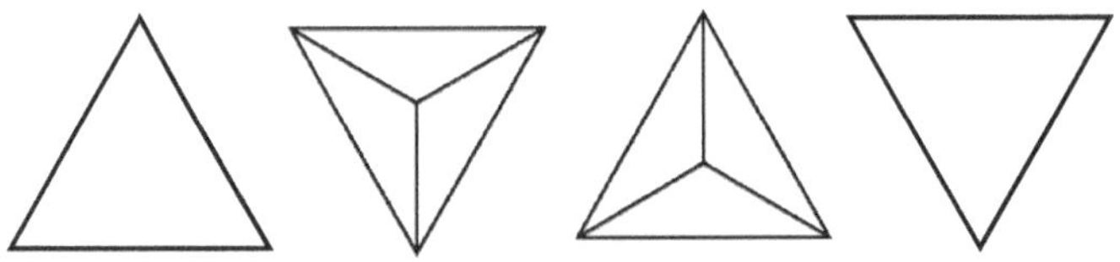

The upward triangle symbolizes the active power of creation and nature. It relates to the fire element, the air element, masculine energy, and the rational mind. The downward triangle signifies the dormant or passive power of creation and nature. It relates to the water element, the earth element, feminine energy, and the intuitive mind. Together, the triangles unite these polarities, and the most harmonized representation of this is the six-pointed star, also known as the Shaktona or the Star of David.

KEYWORDS FOR MANIFESTATION, SHIELDING, HEALING, AND OTHER PROPERTIES:

The upward triangle for inspiration, drive, zeal, and strengthening the masculine energy. The downward triangle for bringing ideas into life, creativity, intuition, clairvoyance, and strengthening the feminine energy. The six-pointed star shape made of two interlocking triangles represents the unity of both.

SIX-POINTED STARS, HEXAGON, AND CUBE

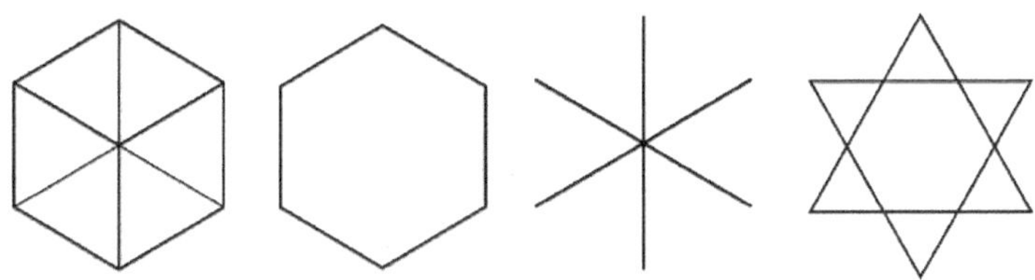

Most six-pointed star symbols derive from the hexagon and its three-dimensional version, the cube. In sacred geometry, these two shapes are the basic blocks of this physical world, as we can see them in the shape of atoms, molecules, and crystals. In a magical sense, six-pointed stars help us materialize as well as sustain our creations. Moreover, these stars have a highly shielding quality.

The hexagram, or the Jewish Star of David, is a symbol of protection and spirituality. In India, the same symbol is known as the Shaktona and represents the heart chakra and sacred marriage.

Their three-dimensional version, the double tetrahedron, has been popularized as the Merkaba, the light body that allows our spirit to shift between the realms and dimensions. The snowflake variation of the six-pointed star (three spikes united) symbolized the World Tree or Tree of Life in ancient Europe.

KEYWORDS FOR MANIFESTATION, SHIELDING, HEALING, AND OTHER
PROPERTIES:

Structuring, bonding, materializing and sustaining creation, shielding, protecting, World Tree, Tree of Life, multiverse, spirituality, faith, sacred marriage, heart chakra, astral travel, light body or Merkaba.

Double tetrahedron/ Merkaba

THE GOLDEN RECTANGLE

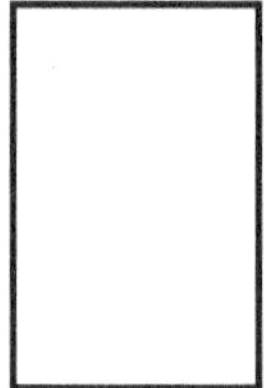

The golden rectangle is a perfect example of a geometrical figure where all the sides are in the golden ratio, the divine< proportion that nature likes to use to create life. This ratio is observed in the growth of plants and the development of animals and humans and is considered the perfect proportion in art. The golden rectangle stands for harmony, creativity, and progress. Its energy helps bring anything stagnant into motion and speeds up the manifestation and healing processes.

KEYWORDS FOR MANIFESTATION, SHIELDING, HEALING, AND OTHER PROPERTIES:

Positive development, progress, movement, creativity, faster results.

FIVE-POINTED STARS AND PENTAGON

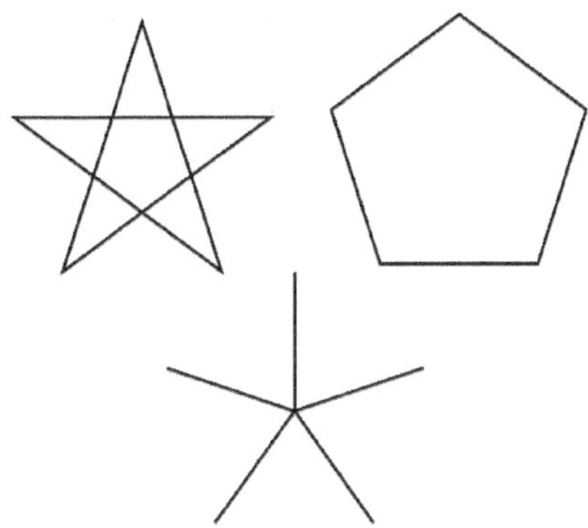

The pentagram and other five-pointed stars derive from the pentagon. They signify harmony, divine proportions, and the human body with arms and legs extended.

Along with hexagons, pentagons can be seen in molecular structures and everywhere in nature and the cosmos. All the pentagon's sides are in a perfect golden ratio, and this divine touch provides it with similar symbolism to the golden rectangle.

Along with the hexagram, the pentagram was part of the Seals of Solomon where it had profound manifesting and shielding powers. In some spiritual schools, it's believed to attract abundance and signify the five basic elements. Among other things, the pentagram was considered a healing symbol, as the Pythagoreans called it hugieia, which means health.

KEYWORDS FOR MANIFESTATION, SHIELDING, HEALING, AND OTHER PROPERTIES:

Movement, improvement, progress, evolution, divinity, eternity, divine proportion, protection, shielding, the five basic elements, the human body, healing, harmonizing, abundance.

Double pentagram doubles the effect of the pentagram.

SEVEN-POINTED STARS AND SEPTAGON

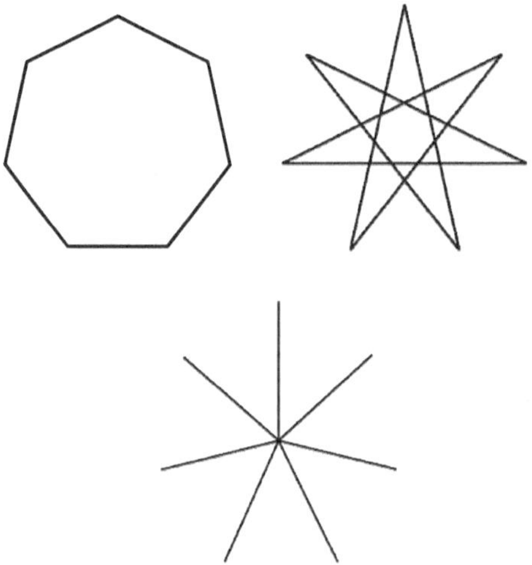

The septagram and other seven-pointed stars derive from the septagon. Like the pentagram, the septagram can be drawn in one stroke and therefore represents eternity. While the pentagram resembles a human figure, the septagram recalls a figure with wings, so it has been seen as the symbol of ethereal beings such as fairies, elves, and divine beings such as angels, gods, and goddesses. Many ancient artworks depict seven-pointed symbols in association with deities. In the occult, the septagram was used to achieve a better connection with spirits, angels, and deities. For this reason, the seven-pointed star helps us align with our own divine selves as well as our spirit guides.

Moreover, the seven-pointed star has been connected to the seven rays of the rainbow, so it also symbolizes the legendary rainbow bridge, which is believed to separate the earthly and celestial realms.

KEYWORDS FOR MANIFESTATION, SHIELDING, HEALING, AND OTHER PROPERTIES:

Eternity, spirit, the divine self, the higher self, benevolent spirit guides, angels, deities, fairy folk, elves, spiritism, channeling, nature spirits, the seven basic chakras, rainbow.

NINE-POINTED STARS

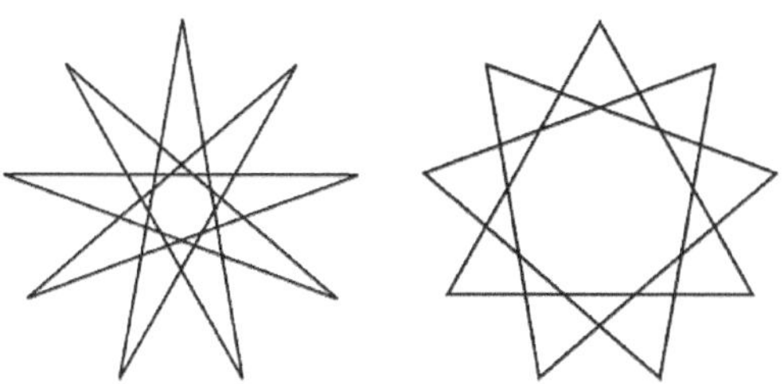

The nine-pointed star is important in Norse magic, as it represents the nine realms of the World Tree. These realms co-exist within the three spheres of existence where the trinity of crown, trunk, and root relates to heaven, earth, and the underworld, or to the past, present, and future.

Overall, the nine-pointed star represents the multiverse and our multi-dimensionality. It helps us understand the various planes of existence, timelines, realms, and their interconnectedness. That's why the star of nine rays makes a great token for channelers, mediumships, psychics, or those who practice astral projection.

Like the septagram and pentagram, the nine-pointed nonagram can be drawn in one stroke, and therefore also represents eternity.

KEYWORDS FOR MANIFESTATION, SHIELDING, HEALING, AND OTHER PROPERTIES:

Divination, mediumship, channeling one's divine self, akasha, astral projection, multiverse, multi-dimensionality, the World Tree, timelines, otherworldly realms.

THE VECTOR EQUILIBRIUM

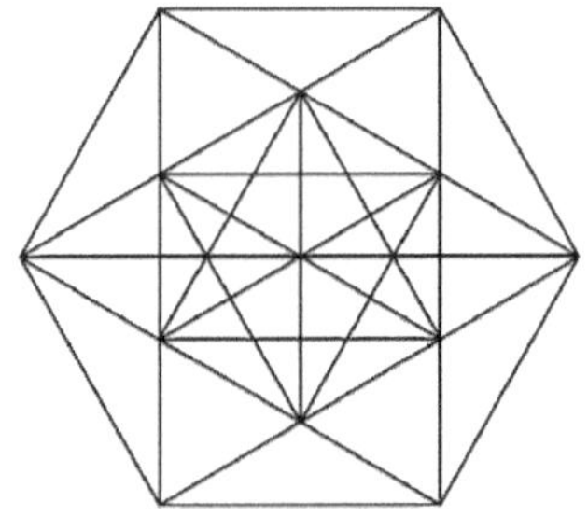

The vector equilibrium is the underlying structure of the torus, the most wholesome geometric shape that resembles the electromagnetic field surrounding everything and everyone. We all have these energy fields, which are produced especially strongly in the heart but also in the brain and other organs. We could say that this electromagnetic field produces the life force of our physical and etheric bodies. It's the source and wholeness of our natural self-organizing, self-revitalizing, and self-shielding abilities. Eastern healing practices call it the "qi field," which is essential in practices such as qi gong, tai chi, and reiki.

The vector equilibrium consists of many geometries, including the golden rectangle, triangle, pentagon, pentagram, hexagon, hexagram, and the Elder Futhark runes. Like the Flower of Life, it makes a wonderful symbol for meditation and contemplation. Gazing at this geometric symbol does something amazing to our minds. It helps us reach a better understanding of our ever-flowing energy field and its healing, manifesting, shifting, and shielding abilities. Furthermore, it helps us understand the interconnectedness of everything around and within us.

KEYWORDS FOR MANIFESTATION, SHIELDING, HEALING, AND OTHER PROPERTIES:

The qualities and abilities of the energy field, energy healing, manifesting, shielding, shifting between dimensions, interconnectedness, unity and individuality, spiritual insights.

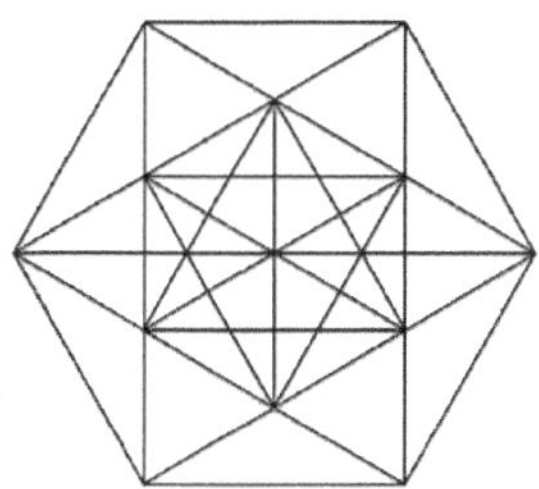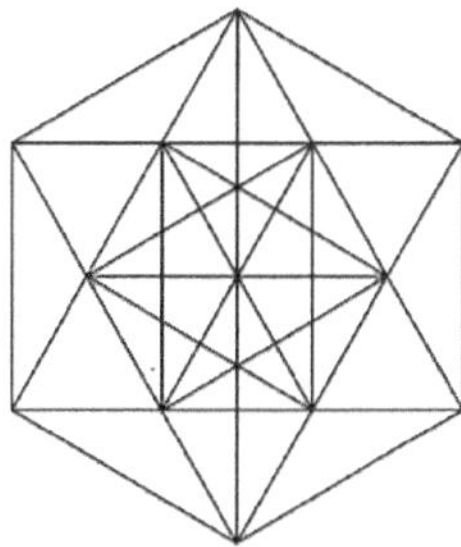

The vector equilibrium variations.

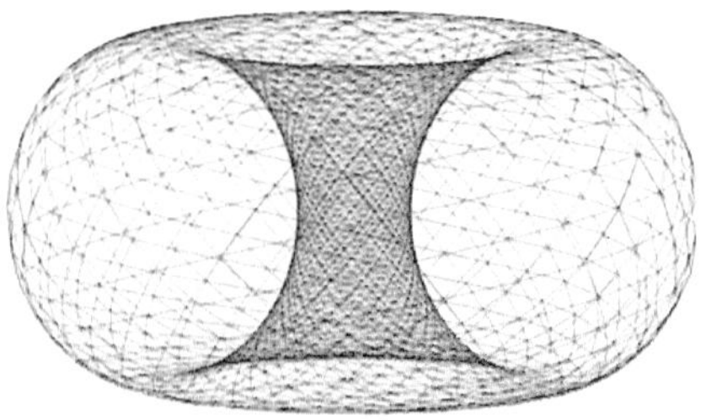

Torus

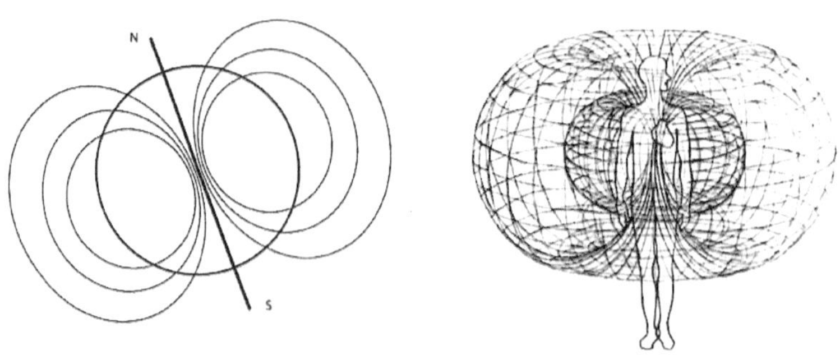

The electromagnetic field of the Earth and of the heart is toroidal.

THE PLATONIC SOLIDS

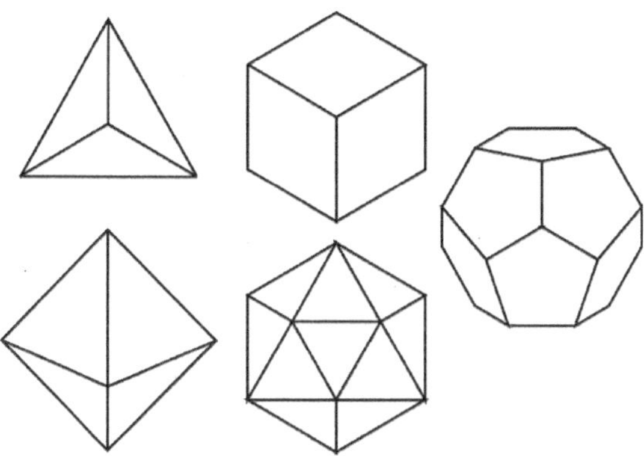

The Greek philosopher Plato considered these five three-dimensional geometries to be the symbolic representations of the basic elements.

The octahedron relates to the air element – therefore inspiration, mental stimulation, and communication. The tetrahedron signifies the fire element – so passion, drive, and personal power. The icosahedron stands for the water element along with its attributes of intuition, clairvoyance, and cleansing. The cube represents the earth element and its grounding properties, stability, and strength. And finally, the dodecahedron symbolizes the fifth element, also called the ether, which is the unity as well as the source.

All the Platonic solids are encompassed in one of the most admired sacred geometry symbols called Metatron's Cube, which derives from the Flower of Life.

KEYWORDS FOR MANIFESTATION, SHIELDING, HEALING, AND OTHER PROPERTIES:

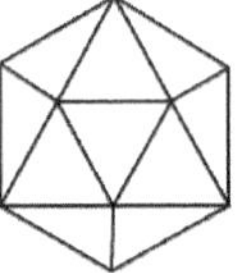

Icosahedron

Water, intuition, clairvoyance, cleansing, rejuvenation, emotional healing, compassion, deep insights, memory, timelines, clairvoyance, divination.

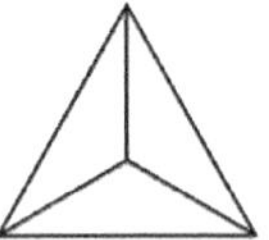

Tetrahedron

Fire, drive, passion, taming emotions, personal power, individuality, creativity.

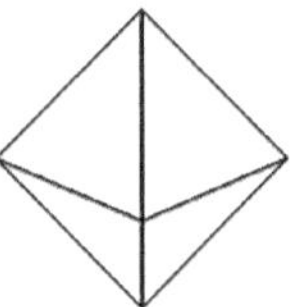

Octahedron

Air, reason, knowledge, ideas, mental stimulation, communication, sharing, life changes, new beginnings, freedom.

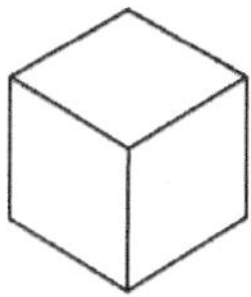

Cube

Earth, grounding, structure, stability, solidifying, revitalization, strength, healing, protection.

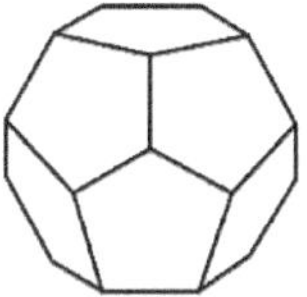

Dodecahedron

Ether, universe, deep wisdom, unity, the all within one, the one within all.

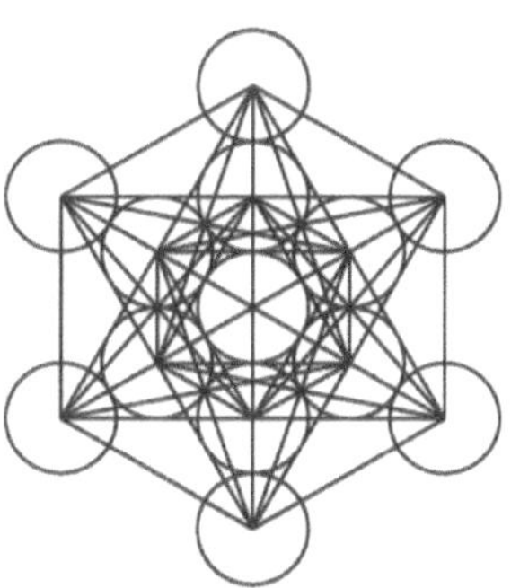

When we connect all the centers in the Flower of Life, we get Metatron's Cube. Metatron's Cube contains many magic symbols and the Platonic solids, which correspond to the five basic elements.

THE SEED OF LIFE AND FLOWER OF LIFE

The Seed of Life (left) and the Flower of Life (right).

The Seed of Life consists of six circles of the same circumference around the seventh central one, while the Flower of Life comprises twelve to twenty-four circles around the thirteenth/twenty-fifth central one. These harmonious geometric symbols have been depicted by many ancient cultures and supposedly conceal the secret of existence. They are believed to be the symbols of this world's driving force and creation.

If we were to connect all the central points of the circles within the Seed of Life and the Flower of Life, we would get all the six-pointed star variations, the Platonic solids, the vector equilibrium, and countless more geometries and symbols, including all the runes. The Flower of Life could be compared to a net, web, or a well of wisdom. It makes a profound meditation symbol, as gazing at it surrounds us with positive vibrations and inspires sudden insights and even breakthroughs.

KEYWORDS FOR MANIFESTATION, SHIELDING, HEALING, AND OTHER PROPERTIES:

Deep knowledge, wisdom, insights, inspiration, understanding, interconnectedness, unity consciousness, the web of the universal mind, the well of wisdom, the secret of existence, possibly the blueprint of creation.

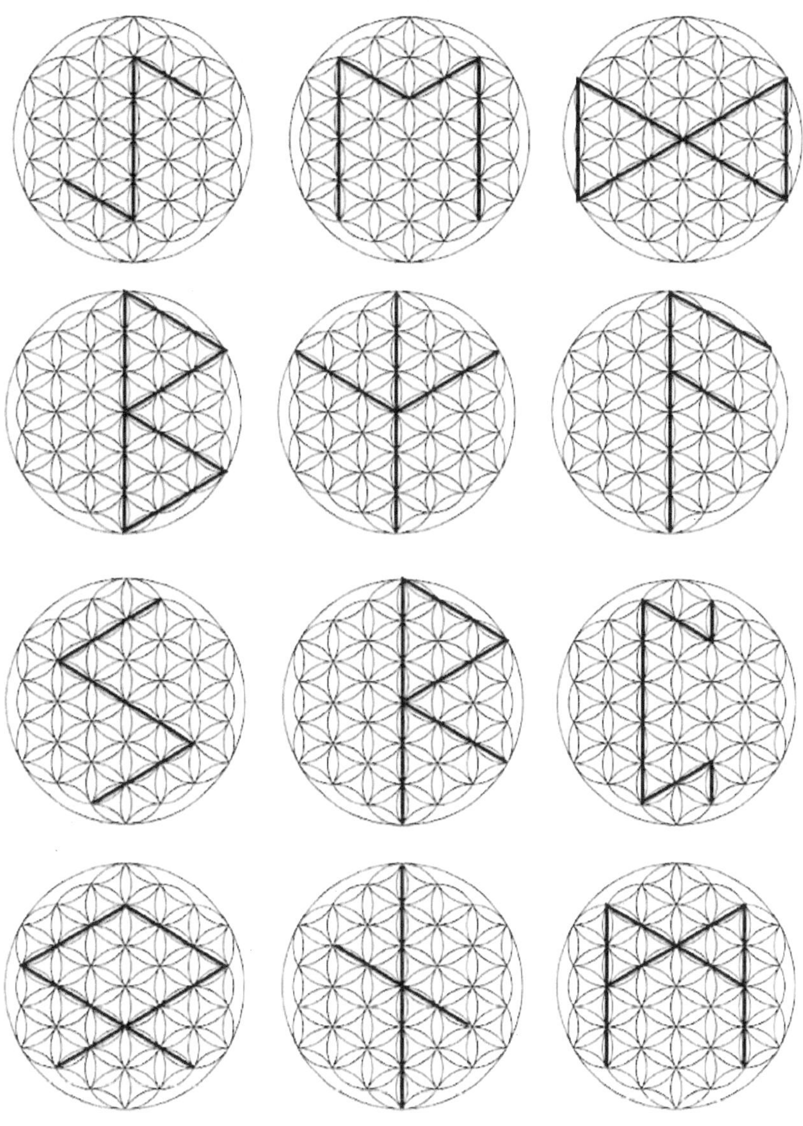

The Flower of Life contains many magic symbols and the oldest set of runes – the Elder Futhark.

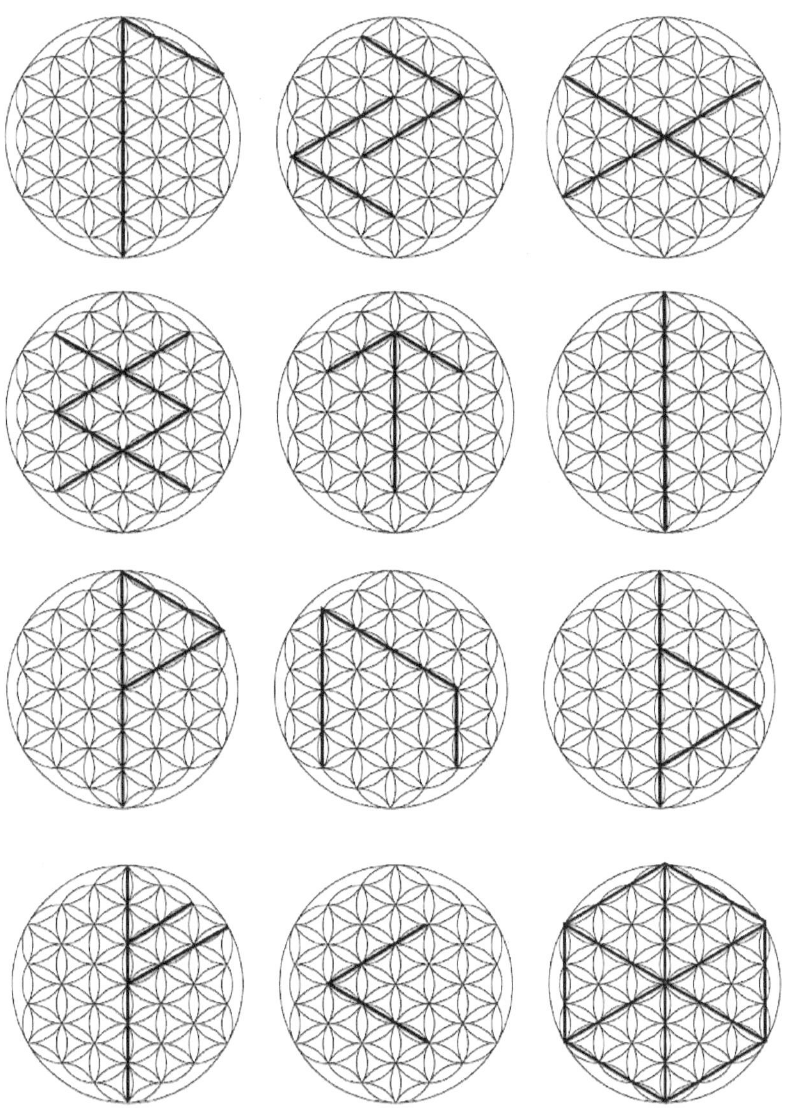

The Flower of Life contains many magic symbols and the oldest set of runes – the Elder Futhark.

THE FIGURE OF EIGHT

The figure of eight can be drawn in one stroke, so it represents eternity and endless possibilities. It resembles the flow of our life force produced in our electromagnetic field, also known as the energy or qi field. Furthermore, it signifies harmony, balance, unity, rejuvenation, revitalization, and energy healing. It has often been associated with serpent symbolism, hence the ouroboros – the snake biting its own tail – and the DNA double helix.

KEYWORDS FOR MANIFESTATION, SHIELDING, HEALING, AND OTHER PROPERTIES:

Eternity, energy flow, flow of the electromagnetic field (therefore energy field), ceaseless possibilities, harmony, balance, unity, rejuvenation, revitalization, energy healing.

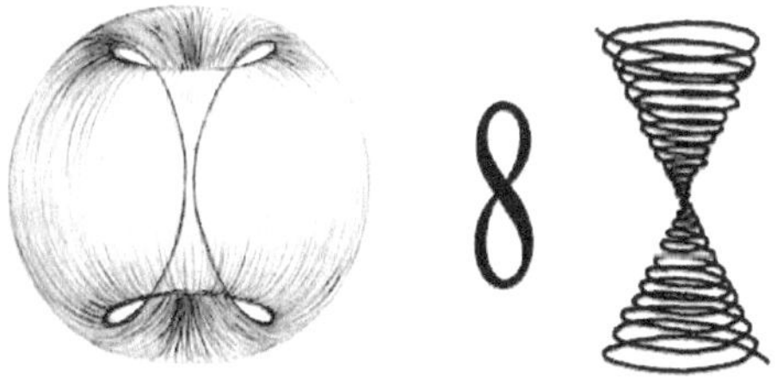

The central vortex of the torus – a whirling, spiraling double cone, which also resembles the figure-of-eight symbol.

THE RUNES

In Old Norse, *rúnar* means "secret consultation," in Irish and Gaelic, *rún* translates as "a mysterious secret," and in Proto-Germanic, *runen* is "to whisper." The runes supposedly come from ancient European cultures – mainly the Germanic, Anglo-Saxon, and Norse tribes – but most historians agree that they are much more ancient.

The runes were not only a writing system but also magic symbols used for divination, manifestation, shielding, and healing. All the runes can be derived from the six-fold pattern of the hexagon, hexagram, or the snowflake version of the six-pointed star, which represents the Norse World Tree called the Yggdrasil.

All the Elder Futhark runes derive from the hexagon/hexagram.

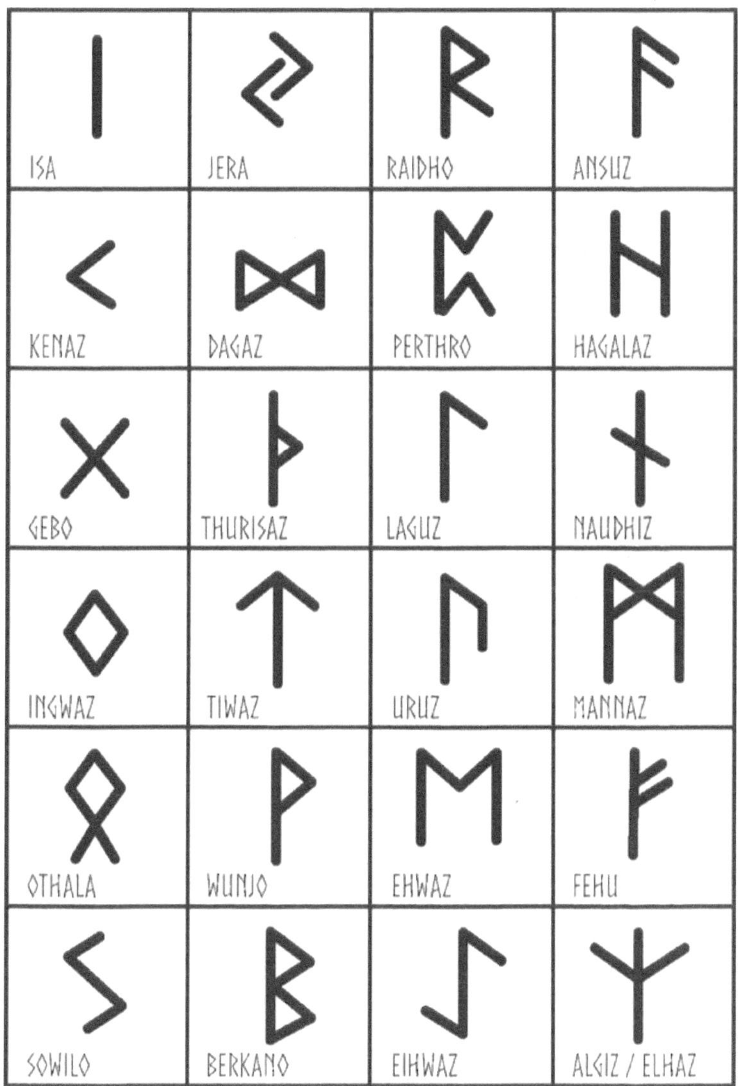

The Elder Futhark runes.

KEYWORDS FOR MANIFESTATION, SHIELDING, HEALING, AND OTHER PROPERTIES:

Rune Isa

The central point, center, the source, the magical wand or staff, stillness, freezing, withdrawal, occasional stagnation, meditation, deep contemplation, individuality and integration, concentration, inner world, the power of now.

Rune Kenaz

Fire, torch, inner light, enlightenment, inspiration, ambition, drive, enthusiasm, creating, being a co-creator in the created world, support of life and light, following our vocation, spiritual path, creative powers, light being, light worker.

Rune Gebo

Spiritual gifts, immediate protection and shielding, sacred marriage, animus and anima, romantic connection, deep and meaningful partnership, marriage, connecting with spirit guides and deities, harmonizing the giving and receiving patterns.

Rune Naudhiz

This rune is not suitable for binding, as it attracts need and struggle.

Rune Laguz

Water, cleansing, rejuvenation, motion and progress, inner sight or the third eye, vitality, emotional healing, divination, divine initiation, mediumship, the cosmos, bringing things to life, the process of creation, regeneration, and recuperation.

Rune Eihwaz

World Tree of Life, timelines, dimensions, endurance, hardiness, vitality, longevity, inner strength, protection, shielding, unity, the power of togetherness, immortality, the trinity of life, death, and rebirth.

Rune Ehwaz

Heavenly chariots, soul journeying, interdimensional and time travel, the light vehicle, the mystery of the Merkaba, the interconnectedness of life within the Yggdrasil (World Tree) realms, astral journeys.

Rune Dagaz

Day and night, recent situations or events, the sun and moon, light and shadow, the conscious and unconscious mind, inner and outer worlds, light and shadow aspects, balancing polarities, self-restoring, reflections, understanding inner dualities, near future, yesterday, today, tomorrow, daily sun cycles.

Rune Thurisaz

Psychic protection, shielding, inner warrior, bouncing off detrimental forces, banishing negative energies, releasing curses, good versus evil, inner strength, the power of saying "no," standing one's ground.

Rune Othala

Property, home, real estate, homeland, financial prosperity, roots, clan, family and family ties, kin, ancestry, lifting family karma, ancestral spirit guides, original home of your soul.

Rune Fehu

Money, finance, prosperity, responsibility, property, work, career, abundance on all levels, a healthy and purposeful relationship with money, successful accomplishments, nature's deities, elves, and fairies.

Rune Tiwaz

Confidence, courage, integrity, sacrifice, humility, law and order, cosmic law, justice, self-esteem, inner warrior, bravery, focus on a goal, pursuit of dreams, drive and vitality, the ability to stand up for ourselves or others.

Rune Wunjo

Bliss, happiness, optimism, joy, inner child, love, true heart's calling, rapture, ecstasy, the here and now, simple pleasures, good news, hope, positive changes, active rest, harmony, joyful reunions, celebrations, animals, nature.

Rune Berkano

Mother Nature, goddess, grace and beauty, revival, rejuvenation, new start, new cycles, divine feminine, connecting with the inner goddess, fertility, motherhood, creativity, inspiration, manifestation, materialization, purity, protection.

Rune Raidho

Journey, travel, progress, change, vocation, moving past obstacles, finding one's life purpose, encouragement, perseverance, drive, goals, dreams and aspirations, life's calling, taking action, overcoming procrastination and limitation, exploring, setting out on a new path.

Rune Ansuz

Spirit guides, protection from ancestral spirit guides and interdimensional or extraterrestrial family, spiritual heritage, origins and ancestry, higher self, divinity, divine potential, spirituality, psychic gifts, spiritual insights, magical and divine forces.

Rune Ingwaz

A gateway between dimensions, moment of clarity, deep insights and
realizations, inner preparation for a new endeavor or cycle, vitality,
fruition, god and goddess union, sexuality, fertility, gestation period and
a consequent breakthrough.

Rune Uruz

Healing, strength, physical wellbeing, courage, grounding energy, the
earth element, manifestation, process of creation, cow-related deities,
celestial goddess(es), motherly care and love, Mother Earth,
rejuvenation, recuperation, stability, strengthening.

Rune Hagalaz

Archetypal polarities, cosmic patterns, heat and cold, ice and fire,
creation and destruction, deep cleansing, renewal, a deep
understanding of a crisis, a sudden crisis that leads to change, a crisis
or catharsis that precedes an emotional healing and renewal.

Rune Jera

Changes, cycles, harvests, wheel of the year, lunar cycles, sun cycles,
cosmic cycles, finding wisdom in natural cycles and their effect on our
lives, good work and accomplishments if done with a good intention
(you reap what you sow).

Rune Sowilo

Accomplishment, power, strength, vitality, courage, inner wisdom, fire and light energy, spiritual awakening, warning against blind faith or spiritual arrogance, empowerment, willpower, confidence, inner light, inner guidance, connecting with the sun's power and the sun deities.

Rune Algiz

Spiritual potential, protection, shielding, divine abilities, spirit guides, deities, channeling and psychic work, intuition, remembering where we came from and who we truly are, divine homes, divine guidance, messages from angels and spirit guides.

Rune Perthro

Creative destiny, karma, action and reaction, the past, present, and future, the three guardians of the timelines and dimensions called Norns or Fates, past lives, regression, seer, fortune teller, astrology, otherworldly dimensions, free will versus destiny, purpose of our life's calling.

Rune Mannaz

Human, humanity, human strengths and weaknesses, human duality, humane and inhumane, individual versus society, human gifts and creativity, humanitarianism, human origins, divine progenitors, gods and humans, divine gifts and talents, group of friends, community.

WORKING WITH THE 100 SUPERCHARGED SYMBOLS

BASICS

There are various methods of working with symbols. One of them is to gaze at a certain symbol and utter a magical incantation, affirmation, or prayer. The intention is key, because when our thought connects with the symbol's energy, that's when the magic starts to happen.

Another great method is to trace the symbols with our fingers or hands. Some of the symbols can be easily drawn, and by redrawing them, our energy merges with theirs. It's important to mention that the drawing doesn't have to be perfect if the vision and thought are there. Symbols can also be approached as talismans and meditation mandalas, incorporated into art, and used in home decorations.

PRACTICAL MAGIC AND ENERGY HEALING

In practical magic, symbols can greatly support manifestation, shielding, or cleansing rituals. In energy healing practices such as reiki, we can combine them with other healing symbols. Moreover, we can visualize them in our chakras and energy field. We significantly enhance the magic of the symbols by visualizing them in our heart center; of all the organs in our body, the heart produces the strongest electromagnetic field.

This electromagnetic field produces an ever-flowing, self-sustaining, and self-restoring life force surrounding everything and everyone. Throughout history, many mystics and healers have taught about the miraculous power of this living energy field. In the East, it's known as the qi field and in the West as the etheric field. It's also the symbolic Tree of Life, the source and wholeness of our healing, manifesting, alchemizing, and shielding abilities.

TAKING INTO ACCOUNT NATURAL CYCLES

When working with the symbols regularly, it's beneficial to consider the solar and lunar cycles. For example, if we intend to begin or achieve something, the best time to work with the symbols would be in the morning and at noon, during a waxing moon, or around and after the winter solstice. On the other hand, when we wish to release something or perform a cleansing, it's helpful to use the symbols in the afternoon and at night, during a waning moon, or around and after the summer solstice.

BINDING WITH THE ELEMENTS

Another wonderful method is to draw the symbols into the basic elements and thus bind them with their energy for specific purposes. We can draw the symbols into the elements physically or in our imagination; both are equally efficient if the intention is there.

Fire enlightens and inspires, water rejuvenates and heals, the earth stabilizes and protects, the air brings about change and mental stimulation, and the fifth element of the ether is the unity of them all.

If we intend to heal, rejuvenate, or enhance our psychic powers, it's good to draw the symbols into the water element – for example, a glass of water or any other body of water.

When we wish to manifest material things, gain more financial stability, or achieve protection, it's best to draw the symbols into the earth element such as the ground, stones, and so forth.

If we seek inspiration, personal growth, and spiritual enlightenment, we can draw the symbols into the fire element – for example, a candle flame or the sun.

And when dealing with communication, inspiration, or change, it's good to draw them in the air element, meaning the air or the sky.

However, the symbols may be drawn into all the elements. By doing this, we unite their individual energies and support the element of the ether that permeates and encompasses everything, including all the elements.

BINDING WITH COLORS

If we choose to draw or paint the symbols as artwork, it's useful to be aware of color symbolism, which can also support our intent. Here's a simple chart of what different colors represent:

White
Purity, unity, wholeness, cleansing, clearing, repelling darkness, new beginnings, completion, spiritual sovereignty.

Silver
Moon magic, clairvoyance, intuition, dreams, psychic works, moonlight.

Gold
Empowerment, enlightenment, strength, spiritual growth, prosperity, abundance, wealth, success, sunlight.

Yellow
Good mood, joy, sunshine, willpower, success, divinity, life's calling, personal growth, personal strength, motivation, support, aligning with our inner creator and alchemist.

Orange
Warmth, comfort, friendship, harmonious work relations, successful work meetings, self-esteem, healing addictions, balancing emotions, success in creative endeavors.

Blue
Meditation, deep knowledge, communication, expression, writing, sharing, psychic shielding, psychic work, boosting imagination, clairvoyance, success in communication.

Purple
Wisdom, astral travel, meditations, spiritual growth, justice, repelling psychic attacks and curses, shielding and protection, avoiding negativity, connecting to the universal mind, aligning with our spirit, receiving guidance from angels and ancestors, akasha.

Red
Passion, drive, spirit warrior, courage, energy boost, physical love, sexuality, personal breakthroughs, standing one's ground, fire.

Pink
Love, tenderness, emotional healing, integrity, empathy, self-appreciation, self-worth, self-care, caring, gentleness.

Green
Connection to vegetation and nature, nourishing, rejuvenation, revitalizing, healing, abundance, wellbeing, attracting prosperity, wealth.

Brown
Grounding, stability, strengthening, materializing, bringing things into existence, earth.

Black
Personal strength, empowering individuality, solving mysteries, deep insights, earth, night.

TO SUM UP, YOU MAY USE THE SYMBOLS IN THE FOLLOWING WAYS:

◊   Look at them while uttering a magical affirmation, incantation, or prayer.

◊   Trace them with a finger, imagine them, or draw them.

◊   Incorporate them into personalized talismans, art, or decoration.

◊   Use them as meditation mandalas.

◊   Draw them into the aura, energy centers, and energy field.

◊   Include them in energy-healing practices such as reiki.

◊   Work with them to boost manifestation or support magic rituals.

◊   Combine them in art or home decorations.

◊   For greater effect, bind them with the elements and take into consideration natural cycles.

◊   Draw them in different colors to strengthen the intent.

THINGS TO CONSIDER WHEN WORKING WITH THE SYMBOLS

Here are some things to bear in mind so that our magical practice with the symbols is as harmonious as it can be:

CO-CREATING IN THE CREATION

Whenever we wish to manifest something, we should bear in mind that we co-create in an already created world. This helps us avoid disappointment when trying to pursue impossible goals.

CAUSE AND EFFECT

"What goes around comes around" – that's the oldest magical law. Therefore, we should be careful about what we wish for and what our true motives are so that we choose wisely. Only when we manifest in kindness and harmony with other beings will we receive the best outcomes. If our intention is detrimental to other beings, we could receive just as much negativity back, whether in this or another lifetime. That's just how action and reaction work.

POSITIVE VERSUS NEGATIVE

When it comes to manifestation and healing, it's best to avoid negative words or thoughts, as whatever we utter is what we invite into our space. It's all about phrasing the affirmations or incantations so that we only attract positive outcomes. Everything negative has a positive counterpart, so instead of saying, "I want to get rid of poverty, fear, and anxiety," try saying, "I invite abundance, courage, and inner peace." However, there are exceptions, especially when clearing, banishing, and shielding because negative energies often need to hear a clear NO. In such cases, "I banish this spirit" or "I clear all curses" is in order.

ALCHEMY VERSUS MAGIC

Sometimes it's impossible to create something out of thin air or make it disappear; rather, we need to alchemize one thing into another. This goes hand in hand with inner work. Sometimes, it's enough to replace a negative feeling with a positive one - for example, change jealousy into understanding or apathy into empathy.

FREE WILL

Especially when dealing with relationships, we should consider that another person or more people are involved, and they have their own free will and co-creating plans. To ensure beneficial results on a spiritual level and remain free of karmic debts, it's best to add the following magical sentences to our affirmations: "May it happen only if it's for the benefit of everyone involved" or "May this be in harmony with the greatest good of everyone involved."

FOLLOW YOUR BLISS AND HAVE COURAGE

Everybody's situation is specific, and different things may apply to different situations. However, trusting one's heart is always the key to success. Sometimes releasing our wishes and remaining passive is the wisest choice, but not if it's fear-oriented. Some of us may be subconsciously afraid to pursue our dreams and choose to be passive instead of making them happen. If something feels right and we really want it, then we should try our best to accomplish it, as then the universe will support us.

As Terrance McKenna once said, "Nature loves courage." Don't let the fear of failure or other insecurities stop you. And to quote another wise man, Joseph Campbell: "Follow your bliss and the universe will open doors where there were only walls." Bliss is the key to our happiness and life's calling.

TRUST TIME, RELEASE, AND KNOW WHAT YOU WANT

Trust that everything happens at the right time. If we keep on wishing for something, have done all we can to achieve it, and still see no results, it may mean that we simply need more time. After all, good timing is everything. It might also mean that we have not released our wish yet. It's best to ask for what we want and leave it up to the universe to decide when and how it happens. The more we obsess about it or try to manipulate its effects, the longer we will have to wait. It could, however, also mean that deep within, we may want something else. It's always good to be certain of our desires and perhaps ask for "this or something better."

GLOSSARY OF RECURRING KEYWORDS

Divine Self and Spirit

When working with magic in general, we connect to the innermost part of our spirit, the divine self, which is also the source of our sovereign creator, alchemist, healer, guardian, seer, and guru. It's good to be aware of that part of ourselves and consciously align with its profound powers to achieve the best results in manifestation, healing, divination, or shielding.

Shadow and Light Parts of the Spirit

Our spirit has its light and shadow aspects. The shadow part tends to be ignored or feared, but even darkness and shadow may have a positive impact. Just as we like to retreat to the shade on a sunny day, so our shadow can support our light, and just as we see the stars better at night, so may our inner darkness unveil unexpected light.

Co-Creator and Co-Creating

This book is based on the idea that we all co-create this world together. And so, while we may manifest our dreams and aspirations, we also need to bear in mind that there are other co-creators in this already created world and that their free will has an effect too, though it doesn't have to be accepted or supported by us.

Life's Calling and Purpose

In this book, "purpose" means the divine self's master plan, while "life's calling" is our spirit's mission for this incarnation, which is in alignment with that master plan.

Multidimensionality and Multidimensional Self

This book plays with the notion that our divine self is multidimensional and has various versions that are sent on different missions throughout the multiverse. The multiverse encompasses ceaseless dimensions and timelines. It could be perceived as the World Tree of Life, the recurring symbol of all ancient mythologies, philosophies, and religions.

PART II

THE 100 SUPERCHARGED SYMBOLS

SUPERCHARGED LOVE SYMBOLS

The following supercharged symbols were created to help us

with self-love as well as love connections with others.

They bind geometries, symbols, and runes that

attract love and bless relationships.

When the free will of others is respected,

they can work magic in affirmations and love spells.

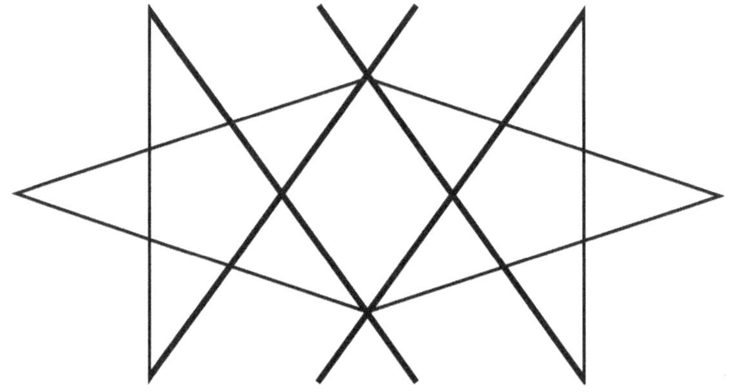

ATTRACT A LIFE PARTNER

This symbol helps us attract a life partner who is in alignment with our spirit and life's calling. It takes an open mind and heart to work with this symbol, as the person who shows up on our path may not be what we consider ideal.

SUGGESTED AFFIRMATION

"I'm now ready to attract a life partner into my life.
With an open mind and open heart, I welcome the person who resonates with my spirit and my current life path so that we may support each other and evolve together."

SUGGESTED INCANTATION

You who are in harmony with my spirit,
You who are in harmony with my soul,
Come, let's share our lives and dreams.
Let's make each other happy and whole.

The symbol consists of the following geometries and runes:

Pentagram

Rune Gebo

Rune Othala

Rune Ingwaz

...and more hidden ones waiting for you to find...

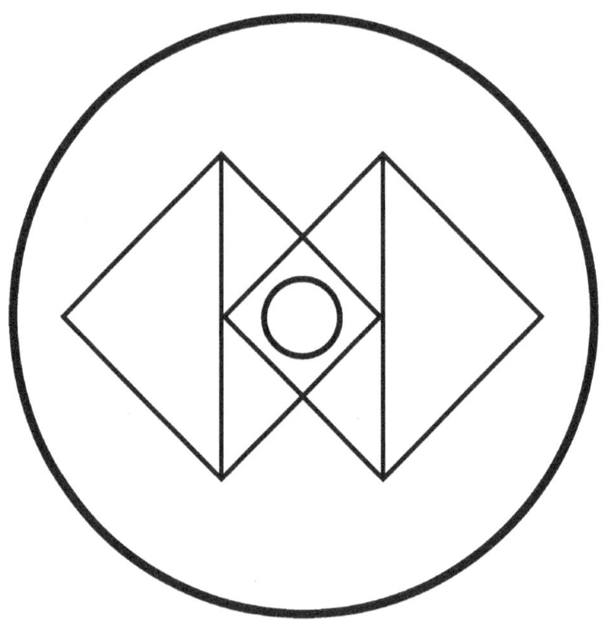

LOVE BOND

This symbol blesses and strengthens a love bond with someone. It can support a blossoming love or improve an already established relationship. Furthermore, it brings luck to weddings, anniversaries, and other romantic occasions.

SUGGESTED AFFIRMATION

"I ask that my love bond with (the person's name) is strong and true. I welcome only the kind of love that is good for me, (the person's name), and for everyone involved."
OR
"I bless this romantic occasion, (name the wedding, anniversary, or similar)."

SUGGESTED INCANTATION

If we are meant to unite,
Then I ask you, symbol, to bind
Our hearts, souls, and minds
So that our love forever thrives!

The symbol consists of the following geometries and runes:

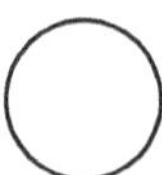

Circle

Rune Berkano

Rune Gebo

Rune Othala

Rune Ingwaz

..... and more hidden ones waiting for you to find…

MIRRORING

Our life partners often become mirrors in order to reflect something important. This symbol was designed to help us understand such reflections. Then, we may find that our beloved's opinions, behavior, strengths, and weaknesses tell us something about ourselves on a deeper level.

SUGGESTED AFFIRMATION

"I'm open to understand what (the person's name) mirrors to me."
OR
"I ask to see what my beloved and I mirror to each other.
I'm open to establishing a better understanding between us so that we may grow from the experiences we share."

SUGGESTED INCANTATION

I'm willing to see
What my beloved mirrors to me.
I'm willing to clear
All haze and misunderstandings.
I'm willing to hear
Even when their lips don't speak.

The symbol consists of the following geometries and runes:

Encircled Cross

Rune Algiz

Rune Dagaz

Rune Gebo

… and more hidden ones waiting for you to find…

CONNECT WITH THE SPIRIT OF A LOVED ONE

This symbol helps us connect with the spirit of a loved one, including beloved animals, whether we are currently separated in life or by death. It supports loving telepathic communication.

SUGGESTED AFFIRMATION

"If it's for the benefit of us both, then I ask to achieve a harmonious connection with the spirit of (the person's name)."
OR
"Please let me know how we can telepathically communicate, my beloved (the person's name)."

SUGGESTED INCANTATION

Love connects, love unites,
Love grows into strong ties.
I call upon you now, (the person's name).
Please, talk to me now.

The symbol consists of the following geometries and runes:

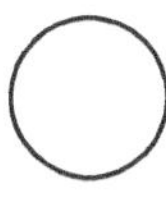

Circle

Rune Gebo

Rune Dagaz

Rune Eihwaz

Rune Ehwaz

..and more hidden ones waiting for you to find..

SELF-LOVE

This symbol helps us release any issues with self-appreciation, as it promotes a healthy love for ourselves. It's also a powerful symbol to work with when we need to forgive ourselves and move on from something.

SUGGESTED AFFIRMATION

"I love and appreciate myself for who I am and who I was born to be."
OR
"I honor my ability to learn from my mistakes and move on from them."

SUGGESTED INCANTATION

I'm empathetic and kind
To my body, soul, and mind.
I embrace myself with gladness,
self-compassion, and self-fondness.

The symbol consists of the following geometries and runes:

Rune Ingwaz

Rune Gebo

Rune Algiz

Rune Wunjo

….and more hidden ones waiting for you to find…

FAMILY HAPPINESS

This symbol blesses a family union and promotes happy family life. It may also help us harmonize our relationships with certain family members, a spouse, children, or animal companions.

SUGGESTED AFFIRMATION

"I bless my family and all my family members, and I ask that we may have harmonious relationships. I'm grateful for my loved ones and want our love to be strong now and forever."

SUGGESTED INCANTATION

Gifts from the divine they are,
My beloved ones, my family.
We are strong when close or far,
Forevermore, I bless our unity!

The symbol consists of the following geometries and runes:

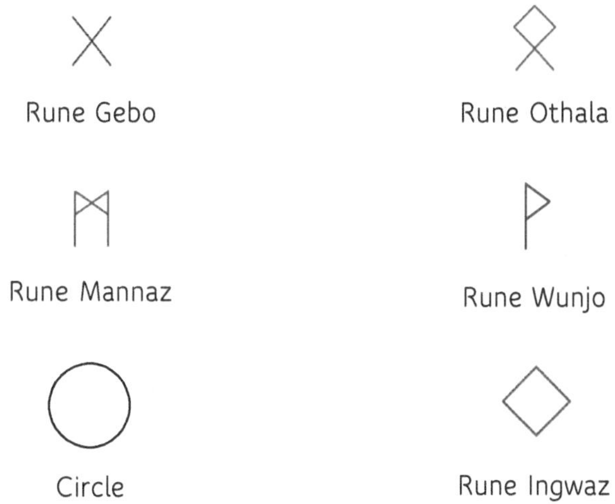

Rune Gebo

Rune Othala

Rune Mannaz

Rune Wunjo

Circle

Rune Ingwaz

..and more hidden ones waiting for you to find..

HARMONIZE AND ALCHEMIZE A LOVE BOND

This symbol helps us harmonize a love bond with someone by alchemizing what no longer suits us into something better. For example, it may help us transmute jealousy into trust, envy into admiration, ignorance into understanding, and so forth.

SUGGESTED AFFIRMATION

"I'm ready to harmonize my relationship with (the person's name) and alchemize any negative feelings and emotions into positive ones so that we know only love, joy, and understanding."

SUGGESTED INCANTATION

My love,
I alchemize what we no longer need
Into benevolent feelings and deeds.
May we have harmony
In our loving unity.

The symbol consists of the following geometries and runes:

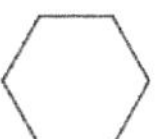

Hexagon

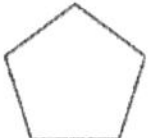

Pentagon

Five-pointed star

Rune Ingwaz

Rune Gebo

…and more hidden ones waiting for you to find…

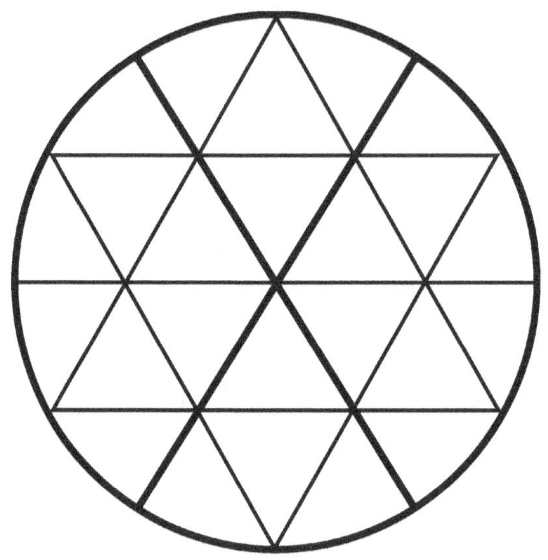

LOVE ACROSS TIME AND SPACE

This symbol helps us strengthen a bond with someone despite being
separated by time, space, or both. It blesses a long-distance
relationship or harmonizes a past relationship that we wish to honor
and heal from or perhaps even re-establish.

SUGGESTED AFFIRMATION

"I am ready to harmonize and strengthen my bond with
(the person's name) across time and space."
OR
"I honor my past relationship with (the person's name)
and heal it across space and time."

I reach across time,
I reach across space,
To let our love align
In harmony and grace.

The symbol consists of the following geometries and runes:

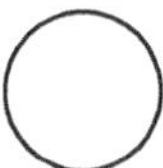

Circle

Hexagram

Six-pointed star

Rune Gebo

Rune Wunjo

..and more hidden ones waiting for you to find..

IMPROVING INTIMACY

This symbol was designed to heal intimacy issues and support a loving
connection with someone on a physical level. It may also help us
release shyness, prejudice, or unhealthy expectations around intimacy.
Moreover, it can promote passion in a relationship that feels too
routine.

SUGGESTED AFFIRMATION

"I welcome intimacy with (the person's name)."
OR
"I'm ready to share my desires with (the person's name)
so that my physical expression of love is healthy and fulfilling."

Unity inward,
Unity outward.
In harmony, with no shame,
I'm ready to fully embrace
Unity outward,
Unity inward.

The symbol consists of the following geometries and runes:

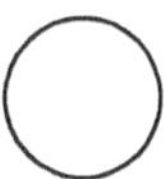

Circle

Five-pointed star

Rune Ingwaz

Rune Gebo

..and more hidden ones waiting for you to find..

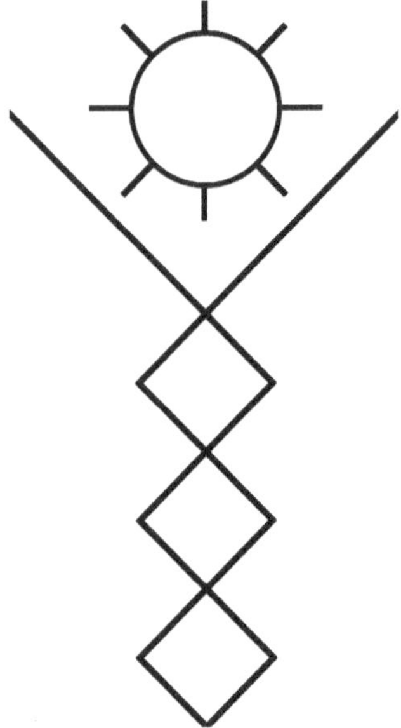

SACRED MARRIAGE

This symbol represents sacred marriage, the symbolic harmony between the divine masculine and feminine. It was created to help us honor ourselves as complete beings and let our inner gods and goddesses shine in unity.

SUGGESTED AFFIRMATION

"I bless the divine unity of my feminine and masculine energies, my inner god and goddess."

SUGGESTED INCANTATION

My inner god and goddess,
You who thrive in fondness,
Teach me about your togetherness,
Teach me about your wholeness.

The symbol consists of the following geometries and runes:

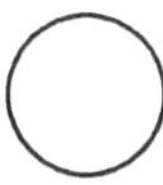

Circle

Rune Ingwaz

Rune Gebo

...and more hidden ones waiting for you to find...

SUPERCHARGED HEALING SYMBOLS

Many ancient symbols, especially the geometric ones,

were considered to be healing.

The same applies to some of the runes,

which can be used in various healing situations.

The following supercharged symbols may be

used like the reiki (energy healing) symbols

and easily incorporated in self-healing processes or

energy-healing sessions.

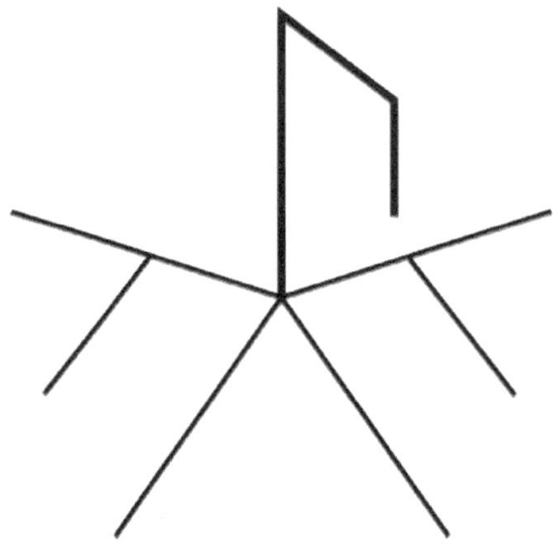

VITALITY AND STRENGTH

This symbol was designed to help boost our vitality and achieve physical, mental, and emotional strength. It's a universal healing symbol that supports energy healing of any kind.

SUGGESTED AFFIRMATION

"I live to be strong and vital.
I thrive to prosper in all areas and on all levels of my life."

SUGGESTED INCANTATION

From my crown to roots,
I feel the energy boost.
From my roots to crown,
May vitality flow all around!

The symbol consists of the following geometries and runes:

Five-pointed star

Rune Laguz

Rune Uruz

..and more hidden ones waiting for you to find..

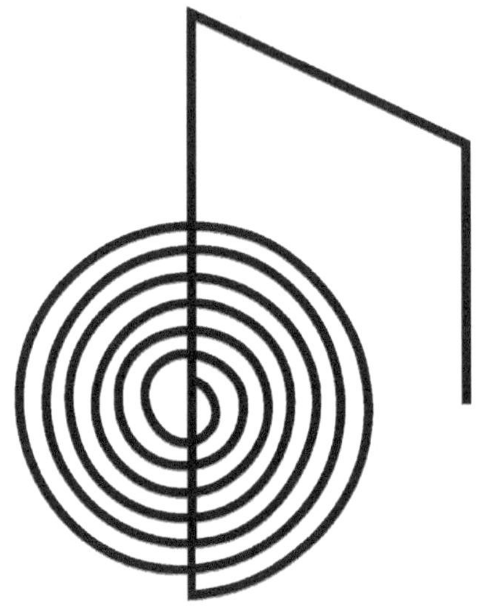

HEALING AND INVIGORATING IN THE PRESENT AND INTO THE FUTURE

This symbol supports energy healing in the present moment and into the future. Meditating on it boosts our energy levels and promotes rejuvenation. It works just as well for animals and plants.
Moreover, it helps revive our environment, so it may be used to enhance positive energy in our homes, in the workplace, or in vehicles.

SUGGESTED AFFIRMATION

"I'm ready to receive my energy healing now.
I program my whole body and mind with health and strength."
OR
"If it's in tune with their spirit, then I now send energy healing to (name the person, animal, plant, or place)."

SUGGESTED INCANTATION

As the spiral spins,
So the Uruz heals.
Spin, Uruz, spin,
Fill me with zeal!

The symbol consists of the following geometries and runes:

Right-turning spiral

ᚢ

Rune Uruz

… and more hidden ones waiting for you to find…

Note: When drawing this symbol, start from the center (inside out) to accentuate the
right-turning spiral.

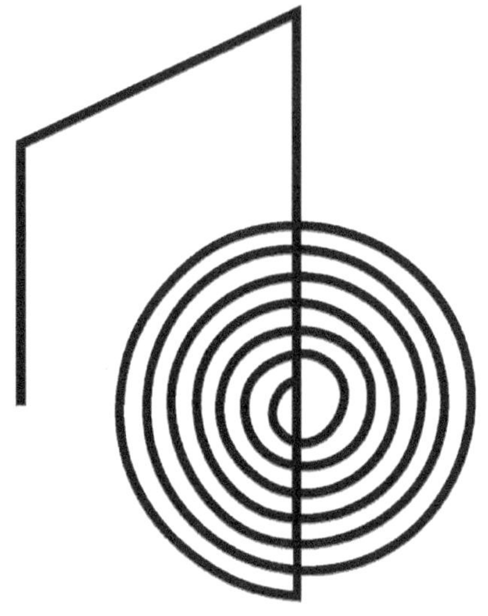

HEALING THE PAST AND PACIFYING

This symbol helps us heal from the past and comforts us during stressful situations. Just like the previous symbol, it works well for humans, animals, and plants. It also has the power to soothe our environment, so it may be used to achieve peace and harmony among family members, friends, or work colleagues.

SUGGESTED AFFIRMATION

"I'm ready to heal my past and set out on a new path now."
OR
"If it's in tune with their spirit, then I now send peace and contentment to (name the person, animal, plant, or place)."

SUGGESTED INCANTATION

As the spiral spins,
So the Uruz heals.
Spin, Uruz, spin,
Fill me with peace!

The symbol consists of the following geometries and runes:

Left-turning spiral

Rune Uruz (left-turning)

… and more hidden ones waiting for you to find…..

Note: When drawing this symbol, start from the center (inside out) to
accentuate the left-turning spiral.

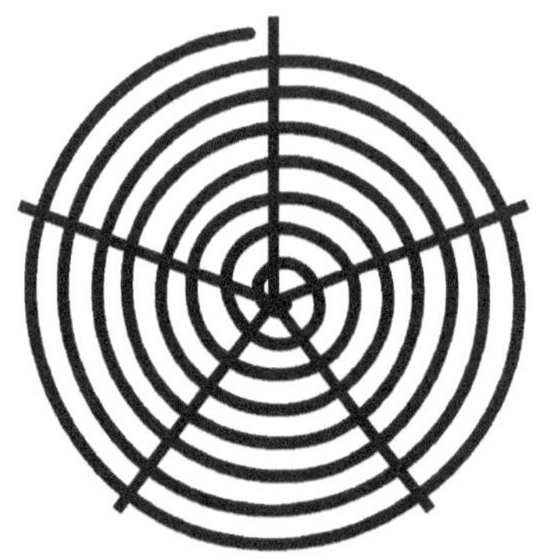

INNER HEALER

Each person has a unique inner healer regardless of whether we practice energy healing or not. This symbol helps us understand this healer and sense what healing methods or techniques it prefers.

SUGGESTED AFFIRMATION

"I now align with my inner healer. I'm ready to perceive how it works and what healing methods and techniques it resonates with the most."

SUGGESTED INCANTATION

Please, my inner healer,
Let me sense, let me feel,
How you work, how you heal.
Bring me vitality, strength, rejuvenation
Through my soul, body, and imagination.

The symbol consists of the following geometries and runes:

Right-turning spiral

Five-pointed star

..and more hidden ones waiting for you to find…

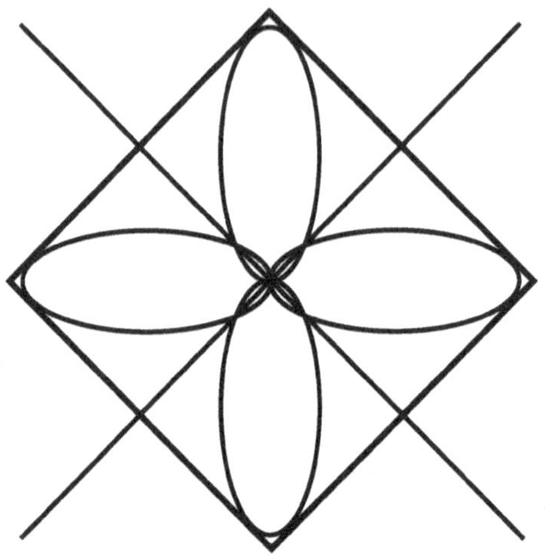

RELATIONSHIP HEALING

This symbol heals a romantic relationship or marriage. It also helps us
to release all hurt or trouble we may have experienced with our life
partner, whether in this lifetime or another.
It promotes forgiveness, respect, and understanding.

SUGGESTED AFFIRMATION

"With the deepest respect for (the person)'s free will,
I now heal our relationship.
I release anything there is to be released,
cleanse anything there is to be cleansed,
and forgive all that is there to be forgiven.
I invite only love and understanding into our lives."

SUGGESTED INCANTATION

Energy flows and unites,
Heals my beloved and I.
Ingwaz and Gebo are one,
United in the power of love.

The symbol consists of the following geometries and runes:

Rune Ingwaz

Rune Gebo

Figure-of-eight (double)

…and more hidden ones waiting for you to find…

HEALING SELF-EXPRESSION BLOCKAGES

This symbol was created to help us heal any self-expression blockages, whether they are of conscious or unconscious origins. It can support us in releasing self-doubt, low self-esteem, or insecurity instead embracing our unique personality.

SUGGESTED AFFIRMATION

"I'm ready to embrace myself for who I am and for what I stand for. In alignment with my divine spirit, I'm ready to express my unique personality to the world."
OR
"I honor my self-expression skills and my ability to use them in the best way possible."

SUGGESTED INCANTATION

My unique voice speaks up,
My personality shines through.
Whenever I fall, I get back up,
Always ready to start anew.

The symbol consists of the following geometries and runes:

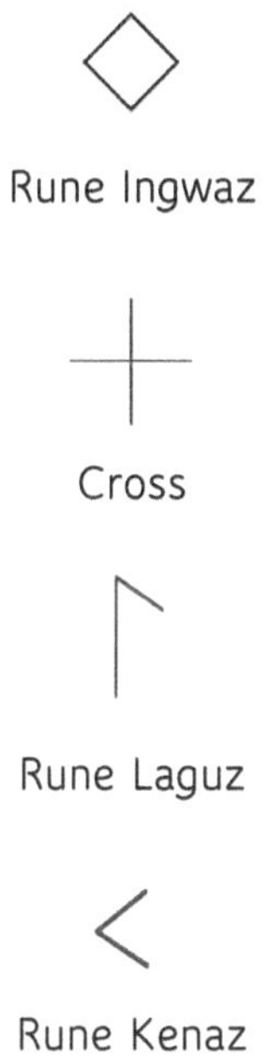

Rune Ingwaz

Cross

Rune Laguz

Rune Kenaz

…. And more hidden ones waiting for you to find…

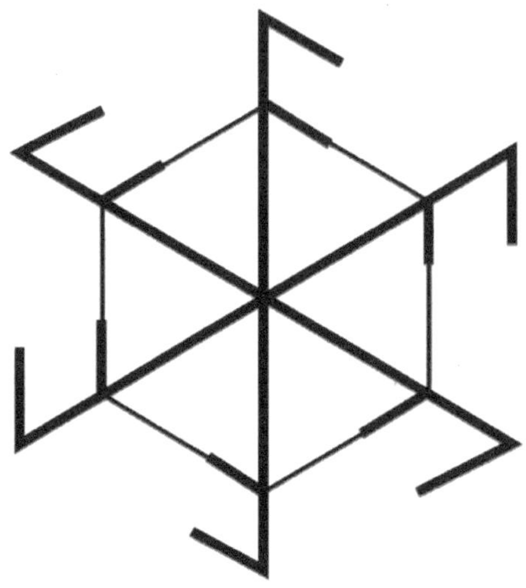

EMOTIONAL HEALING

This symbol heals any emotional issues, whether they're connected to relationships, situations, or trauma. The runes that this symbol contains clear negative feelings, fears, anxieties, and misconceptions about ourselves or others. This symbol may also bring support to someone who is grieving the loss of a loved one.

SUGGESTED AFFIRMATION

"In alignment with my spirit and inner healer, I heal, release, and cleanse the following feelings and emotions: (describe them)."
OR
"I'm ready to move on from (describe the emotional issue) and start anew."

SUGGESTED INCANTATION

Healing I cast
Over that inner flow.
I heal my heart,
I heal my mind and soul.

The symbol consists of the following geometries and runes:

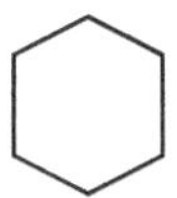

Hexagon

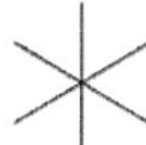

Six-pointed star

Rune Laguz

Rune Ansuz

..and more hidden ones waiting for you to find..

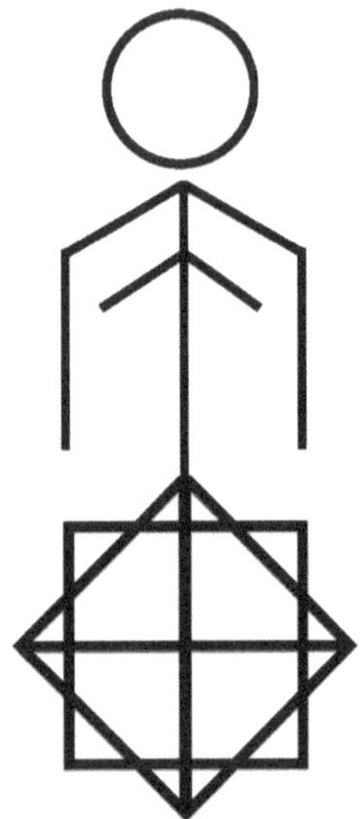

HEALING THE EARTH CONNECTION

This symbol was designed to heal our connection with the earth and nature. It also helps us achieve a better understanding of the yearly cycles, elemental powers, plant life, and animals.

SUGGESTED AFFIRMATION

"I am ready to heal my connection with the earth.
My mind, heart, and soul are open to the wisdom of nature and all its inhabitants."

Rooted in the ground,
Rooted in the sky.
Earth lets me grow,
Heaven lets me fly!

The symbol consists of the following geometries and runes:

Circle

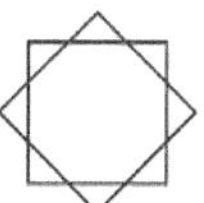

Double square / eight-pointed star

Cross

Rune Ansuz

Rune Uruz

..and more hidden ones waiting for you to find..

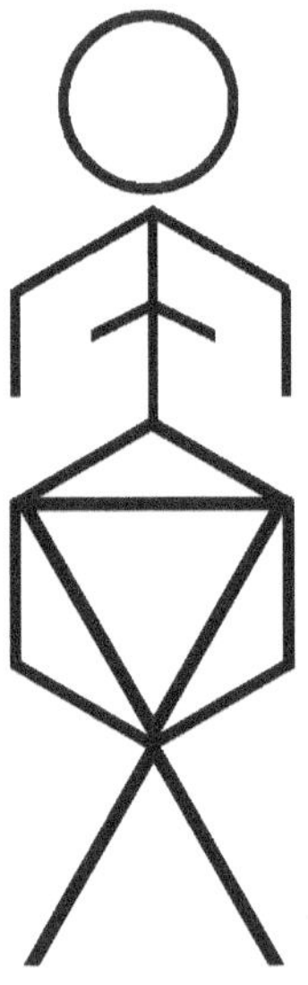

SELF-FORGIVENESS

This symbol heals the feelings of guilt or shame and promotes self-forgiveness. It makes us see that sometimes we tend to blame ourselves for something that was not our fault and not meant to cause anybody harm. However, if it was our fault, then this symbol reminds us that rectifying a bad deed by doing a good deed is better than dwelling on guilt.

SUGGESTED AFFIRMATION

"I forgive myself for all my past mistakes. From now on, my intentions are loving and pure."
OR
"I'm willing to learn from my mistakes and replace every bad deed with countless good ones."

SUGGESTED INCANTATION

After one wrong seed, three good ones I'll sow.
Always willing to improve, forever ready to grow.

The symbol consists of the following geometries and runes:

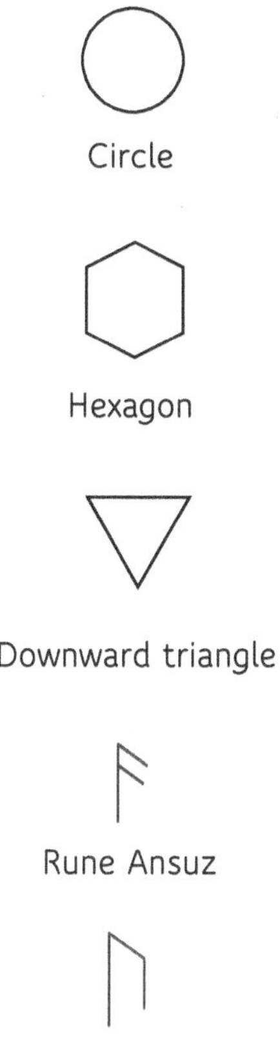

Circle

Hexagon

Downward triangle

Rune Ansuz

Rune Uruz

and more hidden ones waiting for you to find…

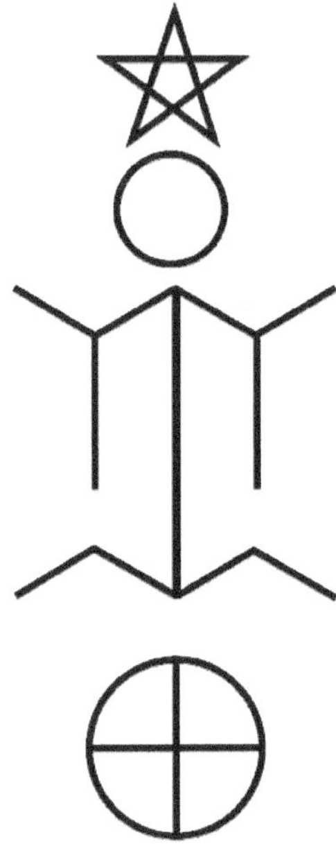

HEALING PAST LIFE TRAUMA

This symbol helps us heal past life trauma whether we remember it or just sense it. It may assist us when we are ready to break all unfavorable karmic contracts and start anew in alignment with our integrity and sovereignty. By doing so, we free ourselves from being slaves to destiny and become its co-creators instead.

SUGGESTED AFFIRMATION

"I'm ready to release all past life traumas (describe them if you are aware of them). In order to liberate my spirit from the bondage of karma, I forgive myself and everybody involved. Furthermore, I clear all negative repercussions these events may have had on my loved ones, others, or me. I break their effects in all timelines, all worlds, all dimensions, by the power of the eternal now."

As the divine co-creator in me awakes,
I clear all past traumas and mistakes.
I heal the past, the present, and the future.
Strength and forgiveness are in my nature.

The symbol consists of the following geometries and runes:

Encircled Cross

Pentagram

Rune Laguz

Rune Uruz

Rune Perthro

, and more hidden ones waiting for you to find…

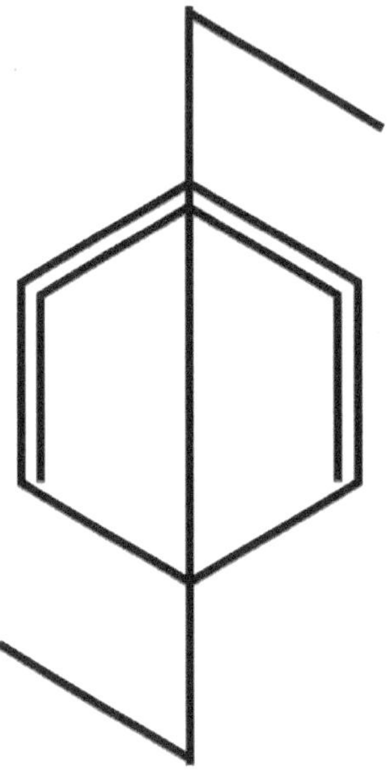

HEALING ON ALL LEVELS

This symbol is meant to help us heal on all levels of our existence and achieve better physical, mental, and emotional states. Moreover, it supports us in releasing any unwelcome emotions or energies that may have come from other dimensions or timelines.

SUGGESTED AFFIRMATION

"I heal myself on all levels of my existence, and in all timelines, dimensions, and realities. My mental, emotional, and physical bodies are healthy and safe in the eternal now."

SUGGESTED INCANTATION

As above so below,
I heal to feel whole.
As within so without,
I heal myself inside out.

The symbol consists of the following geometries and runes:

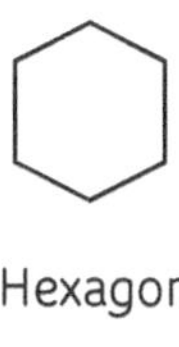

Hexagon

Rune Laguz

Rune Uruz

Rune Eihwaz

.. and more hidden ones waiting for you to find…

HEALING NEGATIVE PATTERNS, ADDICTIONS, AND CONVICTIONS

This symbol helps us cleanse and heal negative mental, emotional, or behavioral patterns. With its help, we may release negative mindsets, convictions, or addictions by replacing them with positive affirmations, open-mindedness, and inner strength.

SUGGESTED AFFIRMATION

"I'm a strong, open-minded, and free person."
OR
"I depend only on my own sovereign intuition and guidance."
OR
"From now on, I will try to create only beautiful thoughts
and manifest a fulfilling, harmonious reality."

Just as I'm respectful and kind to others,
I try to be respectful and kind to myself.
I learn from challenges but overcome troubles,
In alignment with my powerful innermost self.

The symbol consists of the following geometries and runes:

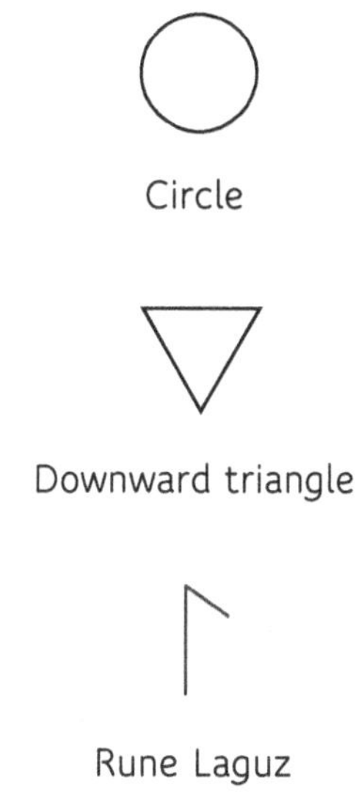

Circle

Downward triangle

Rune Laguz

… and more hidden ones waiting for you to find…

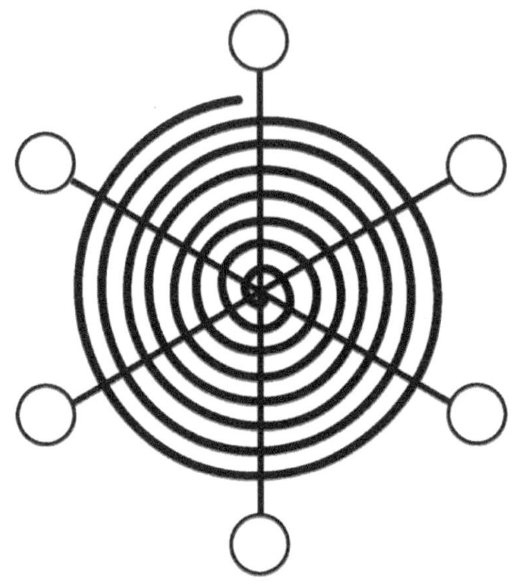

CLEARING, HEALING, SHIELDING

This symbol was created to help us clear negative energies, emotions, or thoughts, but at the same time heal from them and shield ourselves from their impact. It has the power to make us feel comfortable, peaceful, and protected.

SUGGESTED AFFIRMATION

"I'm at peace now: cleared, healed, and shielded.
I reflect this peace onto my surroundings
and my surroundings reflect it back to me."

SUGGESTED INCANTATION

Spin, double trinity,
May all that I don't need fade away.
Spin, spin in unity,
May only harmony come my way!

The symbol consists of the following geometries and runes:

Right-turning spiral

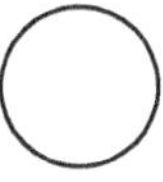

Circle

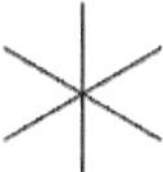

Six-pointed star

...and more hidden ones waiting for you to find...

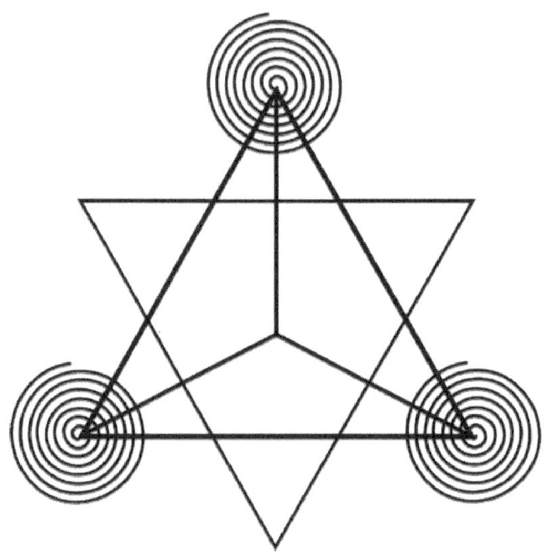

HEALING THE INNER MASCULINE

This symbol helps us heal any issues we may have with our inner masculine, therefore our active and zealous part. It can also promote psychic cleansing of our kin's male lineage, especially from the father's side of the family.

SUGGESTED AFFIRMATION

"I'm now ready to heal my inner masculine and embrace all its beneficial qualities."
OR
"I cleanse and heal my male ancestral lineage.
I let go of all negative patterns connected to my male ancestors.
From now on, I am free and in alignment with my sovereignty."

SUGGESTED INCANTATION

My inner god glows and shines,
In my body and soul it thrives!

The symbol consists of the following geometries and runes:

Right-turning spiral

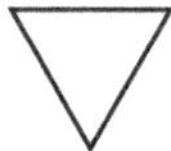

Downward triangle

Hexagon

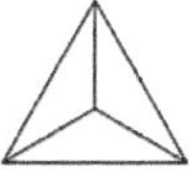

Tetrahedron

..and more hidden ones waiting for you to find..

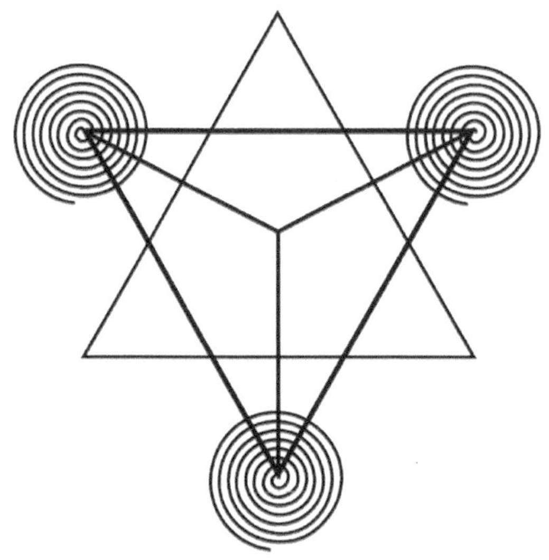

HEALING THE INNER FEMININE

This symbol helps us heal any issues we may have with our inner feminine, therefore our intuitive and sensitive part. It can also promote psychic cleansing of our kin's female lineage, especially from the mother's side of the family.

SUGGESTED AFFIRMATION

"I'm now ready to heal my inner feminine and embrace all its beneficial qualities."
OR
"I heal and clear my female ancestral lineage.
I let go of all negative patterns connected to my female ancestors.
From now on, I am free and in alignment with my sovereignty."

My inner goddess glows and shines,
In my body and soul it thrives!

The symbol consists of the following geometries and runes:

Left-turning spiral

Upward triangle

Hexagon

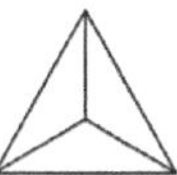

Downward tetrahedron

..and more hidden ones waiting for you to find..

ANCESTRAL CLEANSING AND HEALING

This symbol helps us cleanse and heal the whole ancestral lineage and
release possible ancestral traumas, negative patterns, blockages,
curses, hexes, or karmic debts. Moreover, it helps us cut unhealthy ties
with certain ancestors whose spirits may negatively affect us or feed
on our energy.

SUGGESTED AFFIRMATION

"I heal my ancestral lineage into the endless past and endless future,
in the power of the eternal here and now. I release all negativity,
trauma, curses, hexes, and karmic debts from my kin once and for all.
My ancestors, relatives, and I are safe and in harmony."
OR
"I cut all negative ties with the ancestors who feed on my energy.
I welcome only those ancestors who wish to lovingly guide and
support me."

SUGGESTED INCANTATION

My ancestors and I understand
The chain of our helping hands.
We respect each other's space in order to grow,
As we know well that we reap what we sow.

The symbol consists of the following geometries and runes:

Five-pointed star

Rune Ansuz

Rune Othala

..and more hidden ones waiting for you to find..

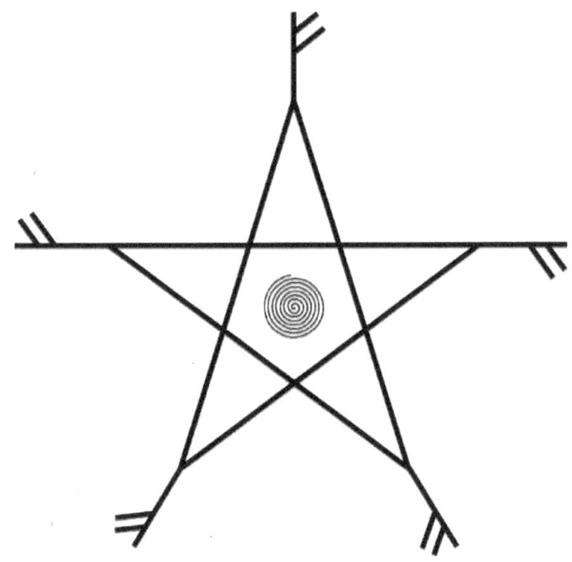

HEALING RELATIONSHIPS WITH MONEY

This symbol helps us heal any inherited or self-induced negative
mindsets about money, whether it's a fear of poverty or a belief that
money is the source of wrongdoing, which may block us from receiving
the abundance we deserve.

SUGGESTED AFFIRMATION

"I release and heal all negative mindsets about money whether I am
conscious or unconscious of them at this given moment.
I'm ready to receive the abundance that I deserve
to live a fulfilled and comfortable life."

I give as much as I receive,
I deserve all the success I achieve.
I receive as much as I give,
In freedom and abundance I live.

The symbol consists of the following geometries and runes:

Right-turning spiral

Pentagram

Rune Fehu

and more hidden ones waiting for you to find…

SUPERCHARGED SHIELDING SYMBOLS

Many ancient symbols and runes have protective qualities,

and the following symbols combine some of the most powerful

ones. They were created for very specific shielding purposes,

such as standing your ground in challenging situations or blocking

negative vibrations, psychic attacks, curses, and wicked entities.

Some of the supercharged shielding symbols were designed to

call in our spirit guides and guardians, but overall, they are meant

to align us with our sovereignty to know that, essentially,

we are our own best shields.

POWER SHIELD

This power shield is based on the Viking bind rune Aegishjalmur (Helm of Awe), which was believed to protect warriors and travelers. It shields us on all levels of our existence and protects the physical, mental, emotional, and spirit bodies. It may also help us to provide shielding for our loved ones, especially when they ask us for help and support, as this will mean we don't accidentally go against their free will.

SUGGESTED AFFIRMATION

"I'm safe and protected on all levels of my existence and in all areas of my life."

Shield my body,
Shield my soul,
Shield my spirit,
Shield me from head to toe.

The symbol consists of the following geometries and runes:

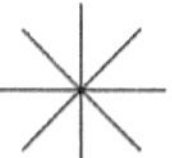

Double cross/eight-pointed star

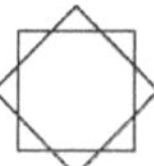

Double square/eight-pointed star

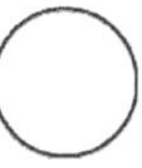

Circle

Rune Algiz variant

..and more hidden ones waiting for you to find.

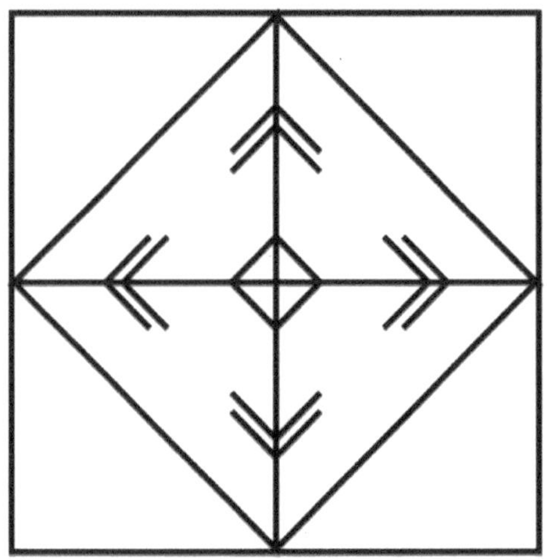

INNER WARRIOR'S SHIELD

This symbol is meant to activate our inner warrior's light shield and ensure protection in challenging situations. It also provides us with feelings of safety and comfort when we need to stand up for ourselves or others.

SUGGESTED AFFIRMATION

"My inner warrior has integrity, courage, and a powerful light shield that bounces back all negativity now and forever."

OR

"I honor my inner warrior's light shield
and know that it will keep me and my loved ones safe."

I ignite that inner spark
That glows through the dark.
I have the courage and might
As my inner warrior is bright!

The symbol consists of the following geometries and runes:

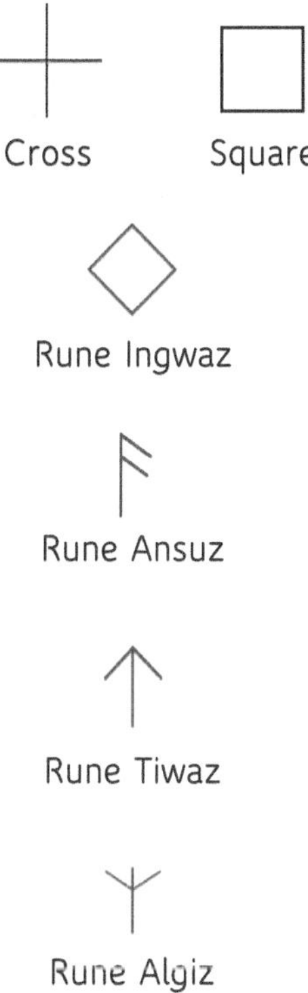

Cross   Square

Rune Ingwaz

Rune Ansuz

Rune Tiwaz

Rune Algiz

..and more hidden ones waiting for you to find..

SHIELDING WITH SPIRIT GUIDES

This symbol activates the light shielding of our spirit guides or
guardians, whether it's gods and goddesses, ascendant masters, angels,
or ancestors. With its help, we can attract their protective energy and
be safe from wicked people, spirits, and any kind of evil entity.

SUGGESTED AFFIRMATION

"I call upon my spirit guides and guardians (name them if you like)
to support my own inner light shield and help me remain safe
and protected within and without."

SUGGESTED INCANTATION

Spirit guides,
Please keep guard
Over my soul day and night.
Spirit guardians,
Please keep me safe.
Help my light shield shine bright.

The symbol consists of the following geometries and runes:

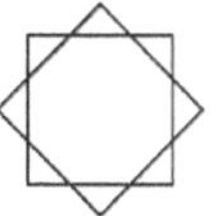

Double square/eight-pointed star

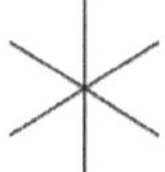

Six-pointed star

Rune Algiz

Rune Thurisaz

..and more hidden ones waiting for you to find..

SHIELDING FROM EMOTIONAL VAMPIRES

This symbol was created to shield us from vampirism of all kinds,
whether it's open or sneaky. It works miracles when someone
continuously drains us of our energy or is directly hostile toward us.
In the case of ill wishes, this symbol bounces all negativity back to the
person who sent them and lets that person deal with their effects.

SUGGESTED AFFIRMATION

"From now on, I welcome only loving beings into my space.
I invite only those who wish me well and care about my wellbeing
as much as I care about theirs."

Just as my soul harbors love and care,
Love and care are welcome in my space.
I invite you who wish me well,
I invite true, solicitous friends!

The symbol consists of the following geometries and runes:

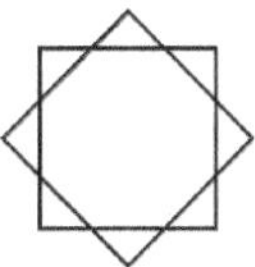

Double square/eight-pointed star

Rune Algiz

Rune Tiwaz

Rune Thurisaz

Rune Ingwaz

Rune Fehu

Rune Ansuz

..and more hidden ones waiting for you to find..

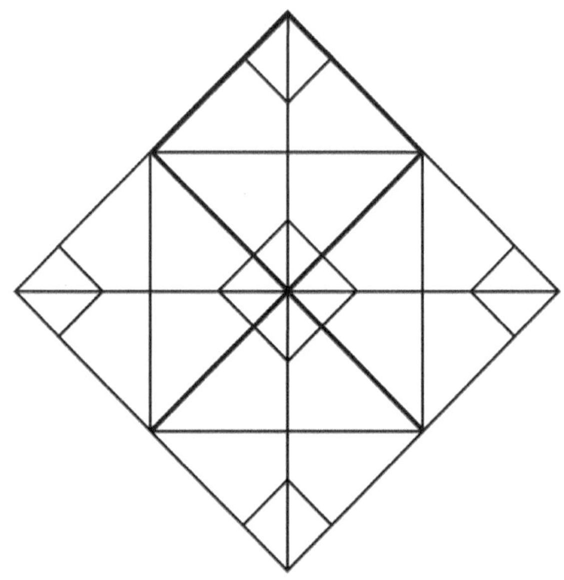

HOME SHIELD

This symbol was designed to protect our homes from unwelcome energies, whether they are envious neighbors, hostile spirits, or harmful electromagnetic frequencies. It's good to redraw the symbol and have it hanging up at home. It blocks all negativity and lets in only positive, harmonious vibrations.

SUGGESTED AFFIRMATION

"My home is safe.
It's my haven of comfort, joy, harmony, and love."
OR
"I hereby cleanse my home of all malevolent spirits, entities, and vibrations. Shooo!
I welcome only the energies that resonate with my spirit."

With this symbol,
I shield my home and its space.
I bless its walls, roof, and base.
I protect it in a light fence,
Oh, bless this grid of defense!

The symbol consists of the following geometries and runes:

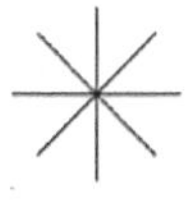

Double cross/eight-pointed star

Square

Rune Algiz

Rune Tiwaz

Rune Othala

Rune Ingwaz

..and more hidden ones waiting for you to find..

SHIELDING ACROSS ALL TIMELINES AND DIMENSIONS

This symbol keeps us protected from harmful other-dimensional energies. Moreover, it helps us remain protected from negative influences from our past and makes sure that we will be safe during challenging future events.

SUGGESTED AFFIRMATION

"I'm safe in the endless past; I'm safe in the endless future; I'm safe in the eternal here and now."
OR
"With the power of this symbol, I'm protected and shielded even beyond the borders of this reality."

SUGGESTED INCANTATION

Across endless time and space,
I welcome only love and grace.
Across endless space and time,
I welcome only that which shines.

The symbol consists of the following geometries and runes:

Hexagram

Triple triangle/nine-pointed star

..and more hidden ones waiting for you to find...

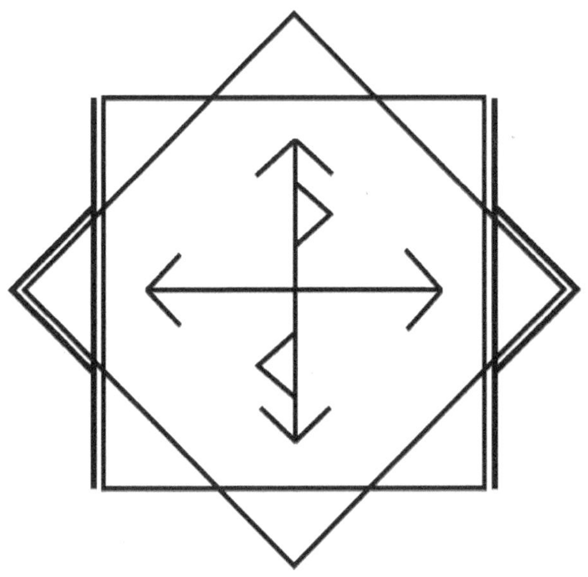

SHIELDING AGAINST CURSES AND PSYCHIC ATTACKS

This symbol repels the evil eye and other types of psychic attacks. It works like a boomerang and bounces back all ill wishes, including hexes and curses. At the same time, it activates the awareness of our profound creative, healing, and manifesting powers.

SUGGESTED AFFIRMATION

"Throughout all timelines and dimensions, I banish all that doesn't serve my highest good. I refuse all forms of psychic attacks. I am the co-creator of my life and know well that I have sovereign power over my thoughts, emotions, and actions."

SUGGESTED INCANTATION

In my divine sovereignty
And in the light of my spirit,
I welcome only positive, loving forces,
Benevolent wishes, effects, and causes.

The symbol consists of the following geometries and runes:

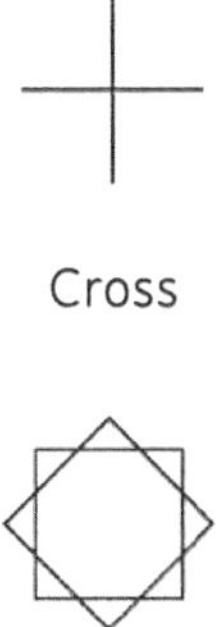

Cross

Double square/eight-pointed star

Rune Algiz

Rune Tiwaz

Rune Thurisaz

Rune Ingwaz

..and more hidden ones waiting for you to find..

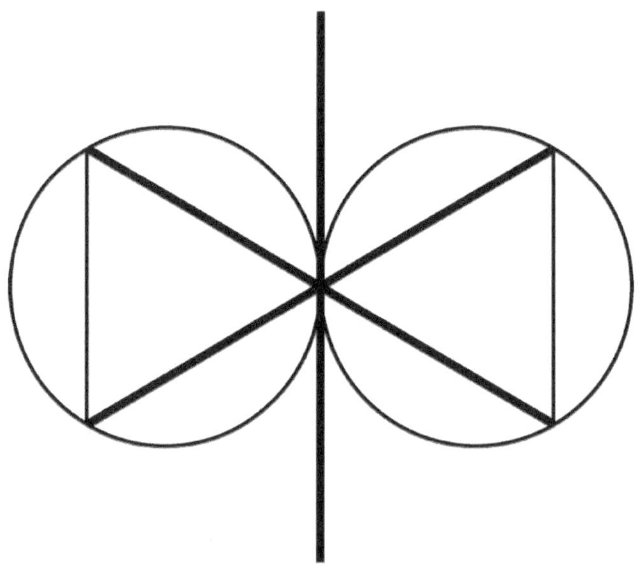

ENERGY FIELD SHIELD

This symbol is meant to protect our natural energy field from all harm,
ill wishes, evil entities, or artificial electromagnetic fields. It works
especially well if imagined around our heart, as that organ has the most
vibrant electromagnetic field.

SUGGESTED AFFIRMATION

"My energy field is shielded and safe. I am whole and protected in my
magnificent self-organizing, self-revitalizing, self-shielding life force
that makes me thrive, manifest, and co-create in alignment with other
co-creators."

SUGGESTED INCANTATION

My beautiful energy field,
Please be my energy shield.
Rejuvenate and heal me,
Support and protect me.

The symbol consists of the following geometries and runes:

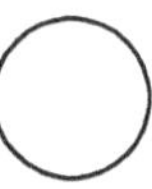

Circle

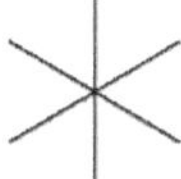

Six-pointed star

Rune Dagaz

...and more hidden ones waiting for you to find.

MEDITATION AND ASTRAL TRAVEL SHIELD

This symbol was designed to shield us from all negative entities and energies during inner-work activities, as that's when we are especially vulnerable. It protects us during meditations, shamanic journeys, and astral projection as well as during sleep, especially if we astral travel in our dreams.

SUGGESTED AFFIRMATION

"With the power of this shield, I'm completely safe and protected during this (describe the inner-work activity)."

SUGGESTED INCANTATION

My mind and soul are completely safe,
Protected in my current time and space.
Shielded I journey, with light and grace,
Safe in all timelines and in any place.

The symbol consists of the following geometries and runes:

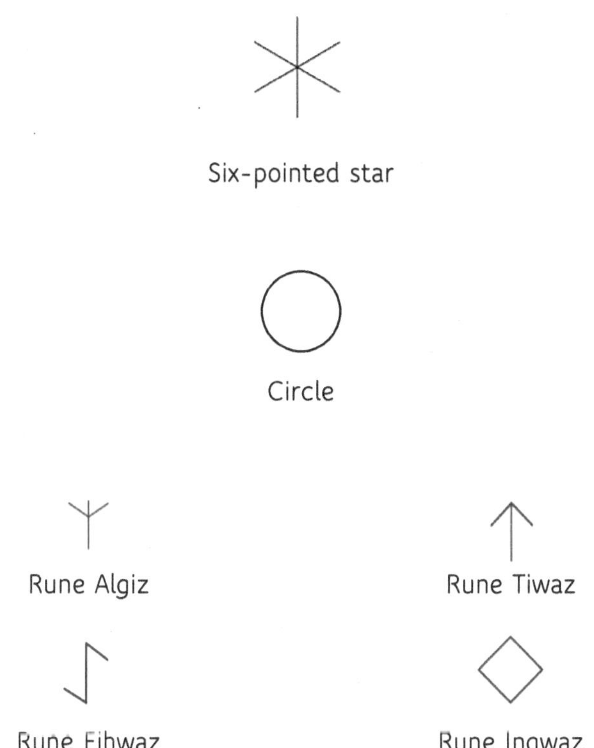

Six-pointed star

Circle

Rune Algiz   Rune Tiwaz

Rune Eihwaz   Rune Ingwaz

..and more hidden ones waiting for you to find..

SUPERCHARGED
SUCCESS SYMBOLS

These supercharged symbols were created to help us find success and contentment at work or in our careers and bring us closer to our dreams and aspirations. They are meant to assist us in various practical situations and balance everyday life with our calling and purpose. Working with them fortifies our connection with the creative, manifesting powers of our spirit.

SUCCESSFUL COMPLETION OF A PROJECT

This symbol helps us bless the completion of a project that we've been invested in. It's perfect for artists or entrepreneurs who want to ensure completion and success.

SUGGESTED AFFIRMATION

"With this symbol, I bless the completion of this project.
May it achieve the success it deserves,
and may it bring me and everyone involved
fulfillment and joy."

SUGGESTED INCANTATION

I bless this project's completion.
As my beloved creation shines on,
May it inspire and impress!
May it have lots of success!

The symbol consists of the following geometries and runes:

Circle

Pentagram

Double pentagram/ten-pointed star

Rune Jera

...and more hidden ones waiting for you to find...

ACCOMPLISHMENTS

This symbol was designed to help us overcome procrastination and achieve great things. It boosts our confidence, inner drive, enthusiasm, and zeal so that we may reach our goals and attain our dreams. It also attracts the kind of success that is in alignment with our life's calling.

SUGGESTED AFFIRMATION

"From now on, I'm a doer. With confidence and excitement, I set out on the path that I feel called to follow and complete my aims and dreams with the passion they deserve."

Rise, my confidence and zeal, rise!
Catch my mind and soul by surprise.
I follow my innermost bliss and vocation,
To fulfill my spirit's purpose and mission.

The symbol consists of the following geometries and runes:

Encircled cross

Rune Algiz

Rune Tiwaz

Rune Sowilo

Rune Ingwaz

Rune Othala

Rune Jera

...and more hidden ones waiting for you to find...

SUCCESSFUL TRIP

Work with this seal to ensure a successful work or career-related trip. It's best to meditate on it before or during the actual journey to bless the whole experience and bring about luck.

SUGGESTED AFFIRMATION

"May this trip be successful, enriching, and fulfilling for me and everyone involved."

A successful trip is ahead,
May my journey be blessed!
May it be a great surprise,
And may my successes rise!

The symbol consists of the following geometries and runes:

Circle

Rune Othala

Rune Raidho

..and more hidden ones waiting for you to find...

SUCCESSFUL MEETING

This symbol is meant to ensure a successful work or career-related meeting. It promotes a good mood and pleasant attitude from everyone involved. It's best to meditate on it before the meeting or take it with you as a talisman.

SUGGESTED AFFIRMATION

"With this symbol, I bless the upcoming meeting so that it's successful and fruitful."

May this work meeting go well,
May our co-operation be swell.
May sympathies be shared,
May positivity be exchanged.

The symbol consists of the following geometries and runes:

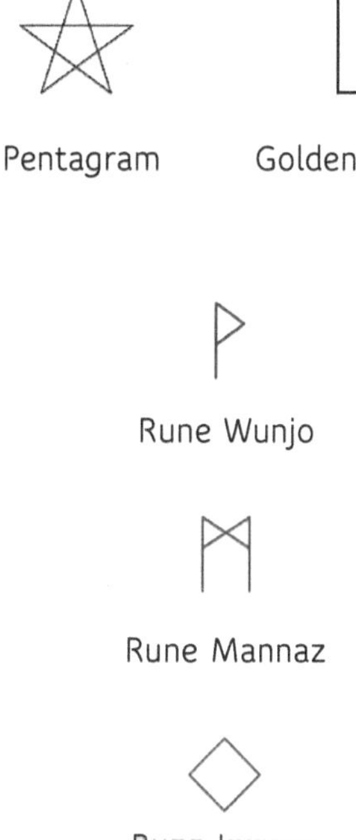

Pentagram   Golden rectangle

Rune Wunjo

Rune Mannaz

Rune Ingwaz

..and more hidden ones waiting for you to find...

ATTRACTING GOOD WORK PARTNERS

This symbol helps us attract good and committed work partners for a
specific project or ensure harmonious relations with colleagues in our
current workplace. Overall, it was designed to invite favorable,
trustworthy, and inspiring people into our professional lives.

SUGGESTED AFFIRMATION

"With this symbol, I welcome work partners that are in alignment
with me and everyone else involved in this work (or project, business,
and so forth)."

I call for kind and sincere companions
Who are in tune with me and my mission.
May we work together well and easily,
May we reach success and prosperity.

The symbol consists of the following geometries and runes:

Pentagram

Double pentagram/ten-pointed star

Ᵽ

Rune Wunjo

…and more hidden ones waiting for you to find…

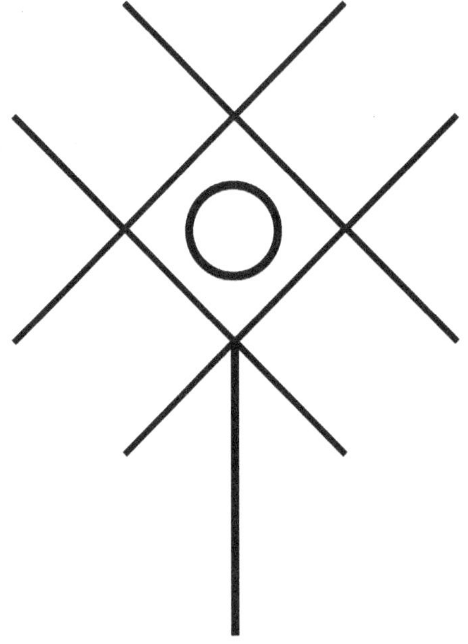

CONFIDENCE IN CREATIVE EXPRESSION

This symbol invites confidence so that we may fully express our creativity and uniqueness to the outside world. It's especially beneficial for shy, overly humble people who wish to be more outgoing and share their gifts and talents with others.

SUGGESTED AFFIRMATION

"I'm a creative, unique being. I'm ready to embrace that and share my talents and gifts with the world."

SUGGESTED INCANTATION

In harmony I grow,
In confidence I glow.
I let my uniqueness shine out,
I let the world see what I'm about!

The symbol consists of the following geometries and runes:

Rune Ingwaz

Circle

Rune Othala

Rune Kenaz

Rune Tiwaz

…. and more hidden ones waiting for you to find…

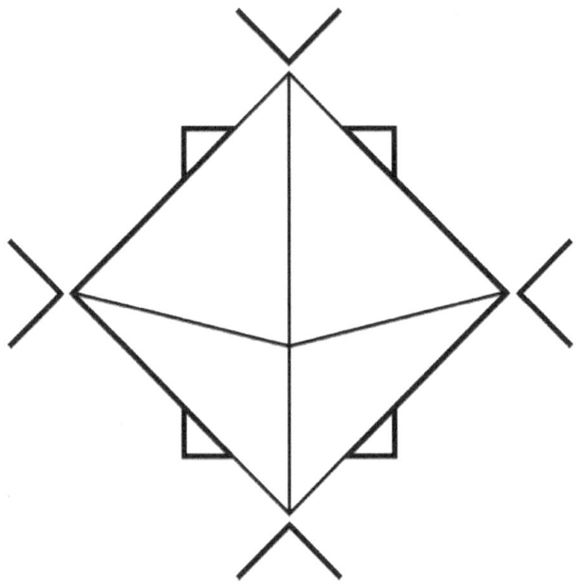

SUCCESSFUL COMMUNICATION

This symbol makes a great token when we need to clear or improve
communication with someone or bless our communication skills in
general. It boosts our verbal competence and can be useful before
work meetings, school tests, or verbal presentations.

SUGGESTED AFFIRMATION

"With this symbol, I ask that my communication with others is clear,
genuine, and in alignment with my spirit."
OR
"I embrace my communication skills and am ready to express myself in
alignment with my integrity, uniqueness, and creativity."

SUGGESTED INCANTATION

I aim to respect and fulfill
My verbal talent and skill
So that I communicate in comfort
And in alignment with my wisdom.

The symbol consists of the following geometries and runes:

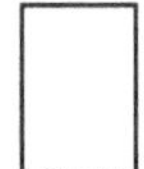

Golden rectangle

Octahedron

Rune Wunjo

Rune Kenaz

Rune Ingwaz

…and more hidden ones waiting for you to find…

BLESSING A NEW PROJECT

This symbol was created to bless a new project and make it happen. It brings about good ideas, creativity, and drive. At the same time, it helps us make sure that our future accomplishments are in alignment with our life's calling.

SUGGESTED AFFIRMATION

"I bless the dawn of this new project and ask that it will be as fulfilling and successful as it deserves to be."

SUGGESTED INCANTATION

Bless this new project and its creation,
Bless my aspirations and expressions.
May I succeed with its realization,
May it reach its desired completion!

The symbol consists of the following geometries and runes:

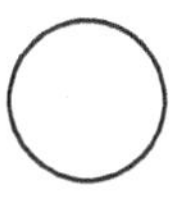

Circle

Upward triangle

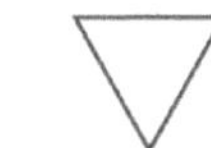

Downward triangle

Rune Ingwaz

Rune Gebo

..and more hidden ones waiting for you to find..

FULFILLING WORK

This symbol can provide wonderful assistance when we wish to attract the kind of work or career that is fulfilling and in alignment with our life's calling. It helps especially well when we are ready to merge what we do for a living with our dreams. It also helps remove any possible blockages that we may have about receiving rewards for our efforts, especially if we affirm to get back as much as we give out.

SUGGESTED AFFIRMATION

"I'm ready to do the work (or build the kind of career) that is in
harmony with my bliss and life's calling."
OR
"I attract only the type of work that makes me feel happy and blessed
on all levels and in all areas of my life."
OR
"I happily accept rewards for my efforts and work.
I let the spiral of giving and receiving run freely."

SUGGESTED INCANTATION

My life's calling is my doing,
My doing is my life's calling.
Always meaningful, always fulfilling,
I happily receive as much as I'm giving!

The symbol consists of the following geometries and runes:

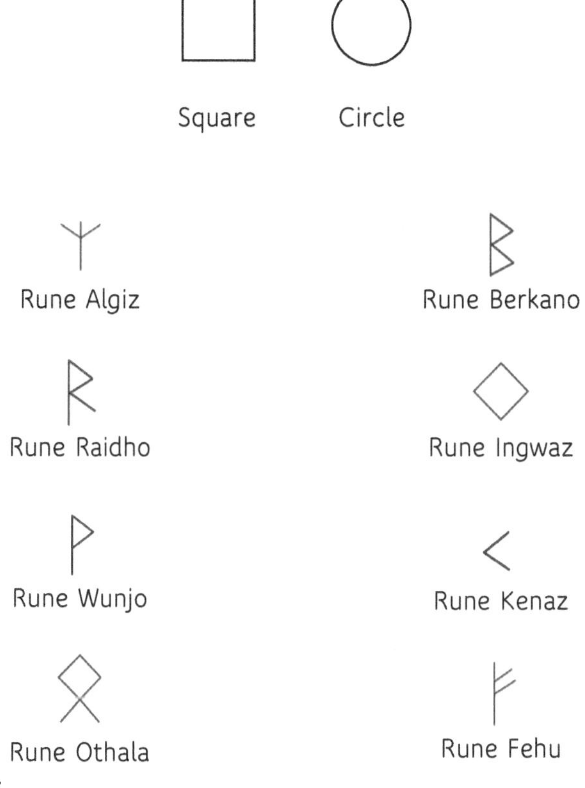

Square   Circle

Rune Algiz   Rune Berkano

Rune Raidho   Rune Ingwaz

Rune Wunjo   Rune Kenaz

Rune Othala   Rune Fehu

..and more hidden ones waiting for you to find…

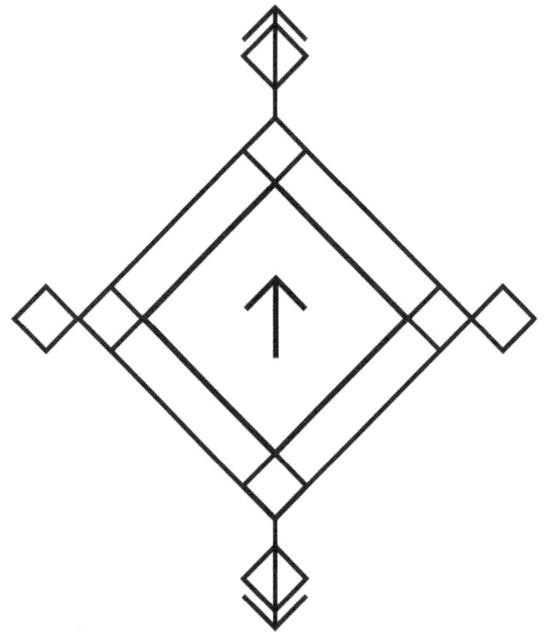

SELF-ESTEEM AND EMPOWERMENT

It's very useful to work with this symbol when we need to boost our self-esteem and empower ourselves. It supports confidence in our skills and talents so that we may freely express them and merge them with our way of life, our work, or our career.

SUGGESTED AFFIRMATION

"With healthy self-confidence, I have a deep trust in my abilities, talents, and gifts. I follow the path of my dreams and live in complete harmony with my life's calling and my spirit's purpose."

SUGGESTED INCANTATION

I welcome wise confidence,
Self-respect and uniqueness.
Aligned with my talent and skill,
I follow my true heart's calling!

The symbol consists of the following geometries and runes:

Rune Ingwaz

Rune Tiwaz

Rune Ansuz

Rune Wunjo

Rune Othala

... and more hidden ones waiting for you to find…

SUPERCHARGED ABUNDANCE SYMBOLS

These supercharged symbols focus on abundance and wellbeing in the material world. They bind powerful wealth symbols and runes to help us attract money, good work, successful careers, or other practical matters such as a dream home or financial support for specific causes.

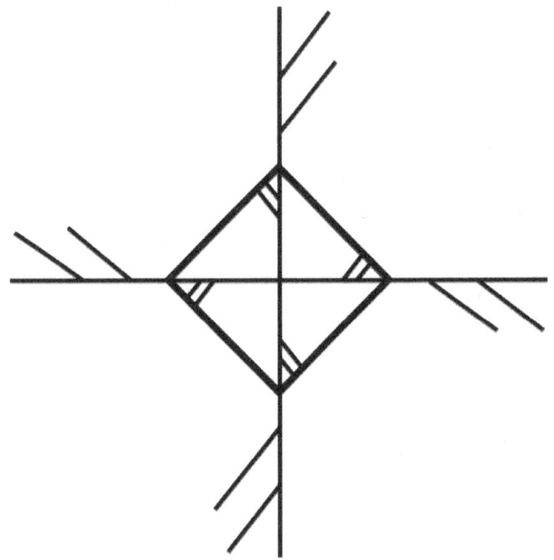

FINANCIAL STABILITY

This symbol was created to help us achieve financial stability, especially when we wish to attract well-paid work or secure finances for our business ventures. It has a grounding and fixing quality to it, so it is perfect for when we wish to manifest a steady income out of something we love doing.

SUGGESTED AFFIRMATION

"My life is now programed with financial stability and security.
I receive financial rewards for what I love doing and what I am meant to do in this lifetime."
OR
"I program my life to have a stable income that allows me to live in the comfort I deserve."

I stabilize Fehu on the north and south,
I stabilize Fehu on the east and west.
Abundance is welcome to come forth
So that my finances are at their best!

The symbol consists of the following geometries and runes:

Cross

Rune Ingwaz

Rune Fehu

..and more hidden ones waiting for you to find..

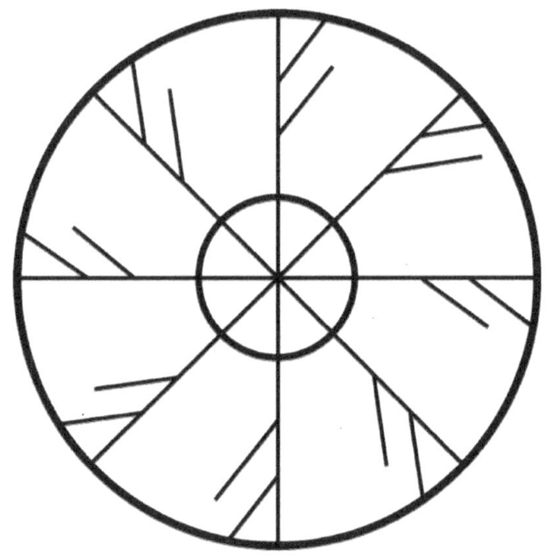

FLOW OF ABUNDANCE

This symbol invites abundance into all areas of our lives. It has a
stabilizing and flowing quality to it, which ensures that our energy field
attracts steady prosperity.

SUGGESTED AFFIRMATION

"I welcome abundance and prosperity into all areas of my life.
May it flow now and forever."

SUGGESTED INCANTATION

Flow, Fehu, flow,
Enrich my life and soul.
Enrich me as a whole,
Flow, Fehu, flow.

The symbol consists of the following geometries and runes:

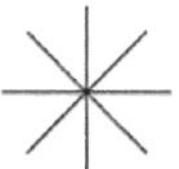

Double cross/eight-pointed star

Circle

Rune Fehu

..and more hidden ones waiting for you to find..

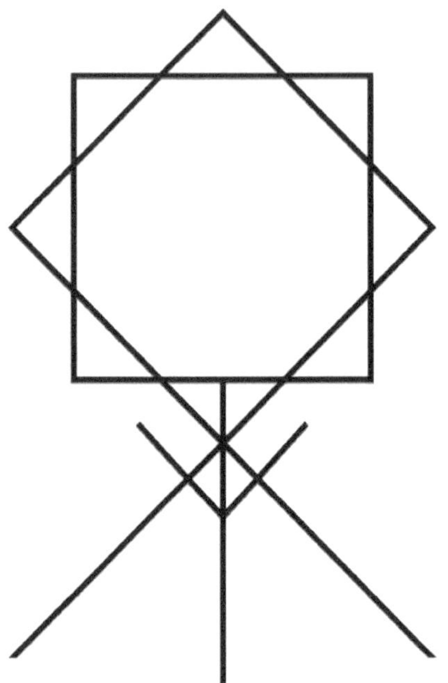

MANIFEST A DREAM HOME

This symbol was created to help us manifest the finances for our dream home. It may set off other signs and synchronicity to guide us to the right place. This symbol may also help us leave or sell a current home to comfortably move to a new location.

SUGGESTED AFFIRMATION

"I'm ready to attract my dream home, and I wholeheartedly welcome all the finances and support that will help me in the process."
OR
"With this symbol, I bless this home for sale (or rent).
I wish to attract good buyers (or tenants) that will live in harmony with this place."

My dream home, tell me where and how
I can find your beautiful haven now.
Please guide me to the right location and place.
Let me live in harmony with your space.

The symbol consists of the following geometries and runes:

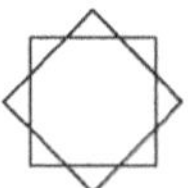

Double square/eight-pointed star

Rune Othala

Rune Algiz

Rune Fehu

…and more hidden ones waiting for you to find…

FINANCIAL SUPPORT

This symbol was designed to help us receive financial support or grants for career advancement, business ventures, or creative projects. It may also be helpful when we need a pay rise or to boost our business.

SUGGESTED AFFIRMATION

"I welcome financial support for (specify the business, career, or project). But at the same time, I ask that the sources it comes from are in harmony with everyone involved."

SUGGESTED INCANTATION

Support and gifts come into my space,
Enrich my life and further my plans.
I welcome you from all possible places
If you come from benevolent sources.

The symbol consists of the following geometries and runes:

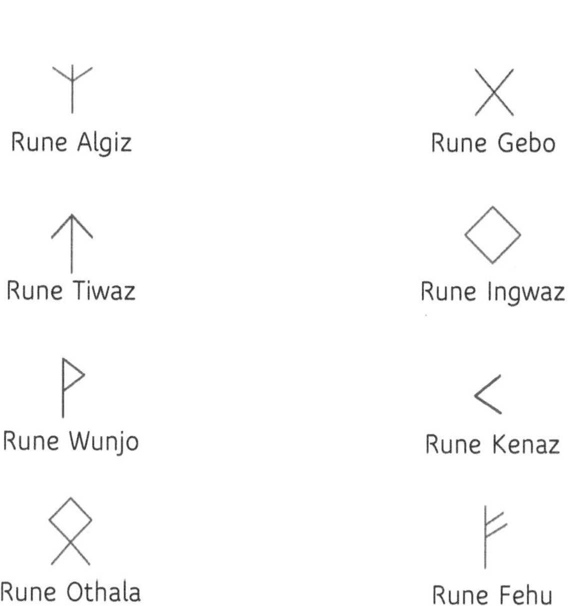

Golden rectangle

Rune Algiz

Rune Gebo

Rune Tiwaz

Rune Ingwaz

Rune Wunjo

Rune Kenaz

Rune Othala

Rune Fehu

...and more hidden ones waiting for you to find...

ALIGNING FINANCIAL REWARDS WITH OUR LIFE'S CALLING

Sometimes it takes time to align our life's calling with our main financial income, but this symbol may help speed up the process. It also helps us receive as much as we give and fully realize that we deserve it.

SUGGESTED AFFIRMATION

"I honor my life's calling and the give-and-receive pattern of the universe. I ask that I receive as much as I invest into what I love doing."
OR
"I ask that my life's calling is always in alignment with my everyday work and financial reward."

As I share my blessings and gifts,
I receive blessings and gifts in return.
My life's calling, my purpose, my bliss,
Make the wheels of abundance turn!

The symbol consists of the following geometries and runes:

Circle

Rune Fehu

Rune Wunjo

Rune Mannaz

Rune Raidho

…and more hidden ones waiting for you to find…

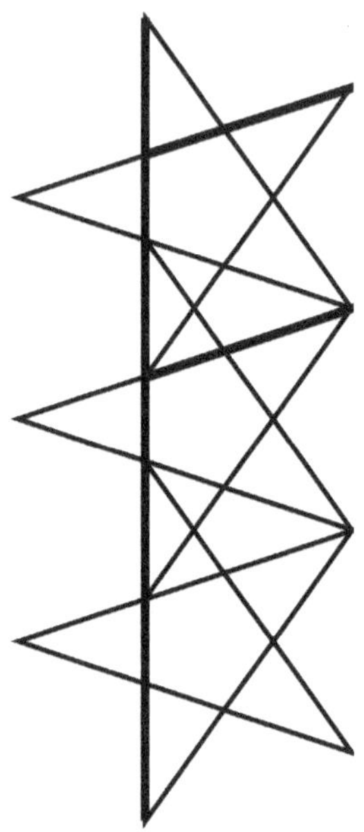

FINANCES FOR SOMETHING SPECIFIC

This symbol can be of great help when we wish to receive finances for something specific such as a charitable cause, a new car, home renovations, a dream holiday, and so forth. When affirming with this symbol, it's good to remain open to the sources that the money comes from, as they may surprise you.

SUGGESTED AFFIRMATION

"I am ready to receive finances for this (describe the specific cause or wish). If it's for the benefit of everyone involved, may it come to be."

SUGGESTED INCANTATION

Come on through, Fehu,
Support this good cause.
Bring me luck, pentagram,
I invite your benevolent force!

The symbol consists of the following geometries and runes:

Pentagram

Rune Fehu

…and more hidden ones waiting for you to find…

SUPERCHARGED SPIRITUAL DEVELOPMENT SYMBOLS

The following supercharged symbols were designed to support us

in our spiritual development. They bind powerful geometric

symbols and runes that help us embrace our natural gifts and

abilities to live to our greatest potential.

They help us attune to the innermost part of our spirit,

the divine self, which is a profound creator, magician,

psychic, sage, and alchemist.

SOVEREIGNTY

This symbol represents our spirit's sovereignty. It's meant to enhance personal empowerment and support us in becoming the co-creators of our reality. Its message is simple: once we learn to master ourselves instead of letting someone else master us, we become the sovereign masters of our life and destiny.

SUGGESTED AFFIRMATION

"I'm my own sovereign master, a divine being full of life, light, and love."

SUGGESTED INCANTATION

My spirit's sovereignty
Is in tune with light, love, and life.
Now and into eternity,
My beautiful, divine self shines!

The symbol consists of the following geometries and runes:

Seven-pointed star

Circle

Rune Fehu

Rune Algiz

..and more hidden ones waiting for you to find.

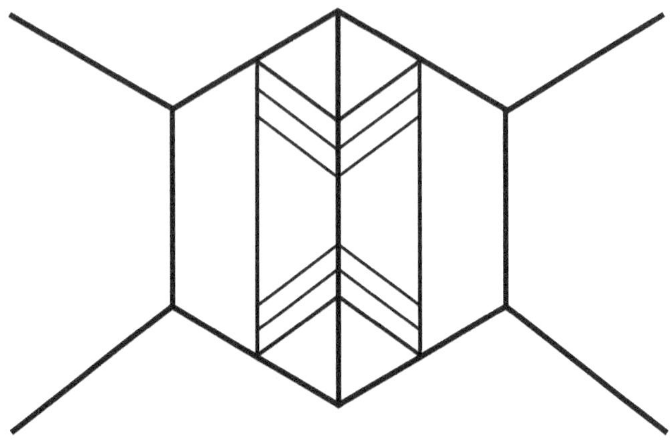

CREATIVE DESTINY

This symbol helps us fix or change something in our fate that appears
to be a burden. The hexagon in the center binds many runes but mainly
Perthro, which is the symbolic representation of the so-called *Örlög*.
This is the Old Norse belief that destiny is not fixed but changeable and
that we can influence it when attuned to our divine self.

SUGGESTED AFFIRMATION

"The innermost part of my spirit, my divine self, creates my destiny.
I know that I can affect and change any present, past, or future
situations to my benefit and in alignment with the benefit of everyone
involved. Therefore, I now wish to change (specify what you wish to
change)."

SUGGESTED INCANTATION

At the center of the wheel
My divine self spins destinies.
It's within where I overcome duality,
It's within where I find my divinity.

The symbol consists of the following geometries and runes:

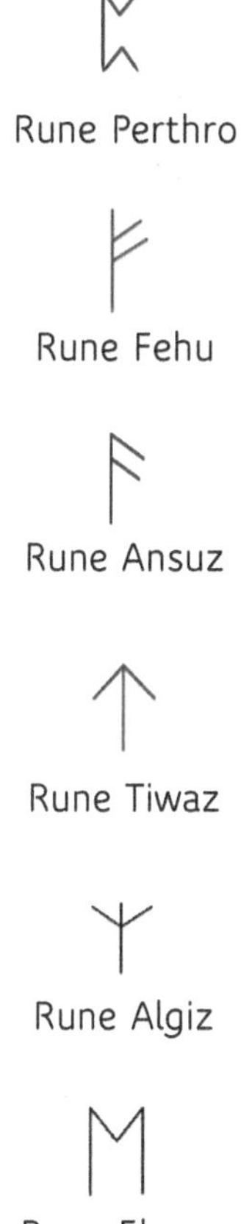

Rune Perthro

Rune Fehu

Rune Ansuz

Rune Tiwaz

Rune Algiz

Rune Ehwaz

…and more hidden ones waiting for you to find.

FREE SPIRIT

This symbol represents the expansion of our spirit beyond the dualistic reality. It's meant to guide us when we want to see past the seeming limitations of this world and unchain our spirit from them.

SUGGESTED AFFIRMATION

"I'm aware of the dualistic nature of this reality, but I also know that I can liberate myself from it and experience heaven on earth."

SUGGESTED INCANTATION

In the duality
I seek liberty.
Mind, soul, spirit – my inner trinity.
In you, I seek the key to divine unity.

The symbol consists of the following geometries and runes:

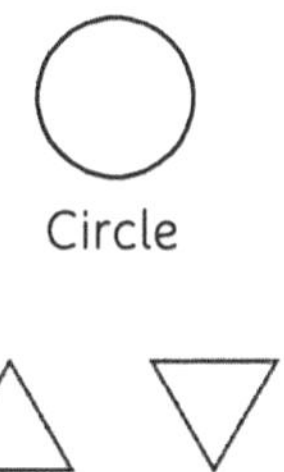

Circle

Upward and downward triangles

Rune Ingwaz

Rune Gebo

Rune Othala

..and more hidden ones waiting for you to find..

LIFE'S CALLING AND PURPOSE

This symbol helps us delve into the core of who we truly are, the divine spark of our spirit, and find out what we came here to learn or accomplish. It is meant to bring us closer to our spirit's purpose, which is reflected in our present life's calling or callings, as there may be more than one.

SUGGESTED AFFIRMATION

"In tune with my spirit and its innermost divine self, I live to my greatest potential."
OR
"I live in harmony with my divine purpose and my spirit's current mission."
OR
"I'm ready to follow the path of my bliss, which is the path of my purpose and callings."

SUGGESTED INCANTATION

The key to my purpose and callings
Is in my bliss and heart's yearnings.
I follow the guidance of that innermost core.
I live to learn, grow, and experience more.

The symbol consists of the following geometries and runes:

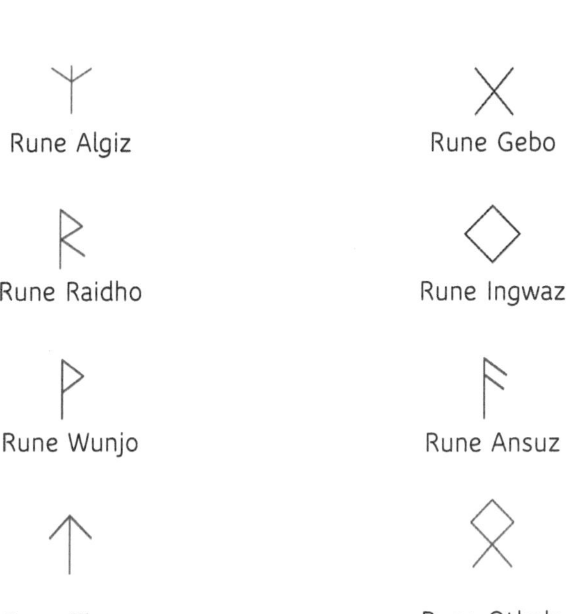

Six-pointed star

Rune Algiz

Rune Gebo

Rune Raidho

Rune Ingwaz

Rune Wunjo

Rune Ansuz

Rune Tiwaz

Rune Othala

..and more hidden ones waiting for you to find.

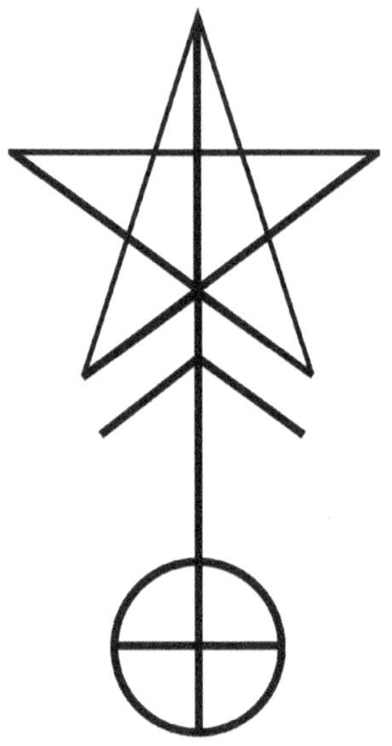

DIVINE ABILITIES

This symbol represents the magical, manifesting, and healing abilities of our divine self that support our physical wellbeing in this world. It was created to help us be conscious of these spiritual gifts and talents so that we may always remain in alignment with our greatest potential here on earth.

SUGGESTED AFFIRMATION

"I'm ready to align my conscious mind with my divine abilities and live in tune with my greatest potential. I enhance my magical, manifesting, and healing abilities now and forever."

My greatest potential I seek,
I trust my divine abilities.
My greatest talents I invite,
To shine through my light.

The symbol consists of the following geometries and runes:

Encircled cross

Pentagram

Rune Algiz

Rune Tiwaz

Rune Sowilo

Rune Ansuz

…and more hidden ones waiting for you to find.

CLARITY AND INSIGHT

This is the symbol to turn to when we need to gain a deeper insight
into a particular situation or wish to resolve something important.
Sometimes it's enough to meditate with this symbol to receive sudden
ideas and breakthroughs; other times, it may attract other signs and
synchronicity that will provide us with further guidance.

SUGGESTED AFFIRMATION

"I ask my spirit for a deeper insight into this situation (describe it)."
OR
"I'm ready to receive more clarity to resolve this issue harmoniously."

<h1 style="text-align:center">SUGGESTED INCANTATION</h1>

I clear my mind and ask to see
What the resolution might be.
I invite useful insights and clarity
So that I may resolve this effectively.

The symbol consists of the following geometries and runes:

Encircled cross

Rune Ingwaz

Rune Gebo

Rune Kenaz

..and more hidden ones waiting for you to find.

TRUTH

This symbol can provide excellent guidance when we need to figure something out or look at a specific situation with the utmost honesty. Therefore, when we affirm with this symbol, we need to be true to ourselves and keep our hearts and minds open.

SUGGESTED AFFIRMATION

"With love and in alignment with my integrity, I now ask to see the truth about the situation (describe it)."

Truth, what is my truth?
Truth, what is their truth?
In alignment with my integrity
I ask for loving, kind honesty.

The symbol consists of the following geometries and runes:

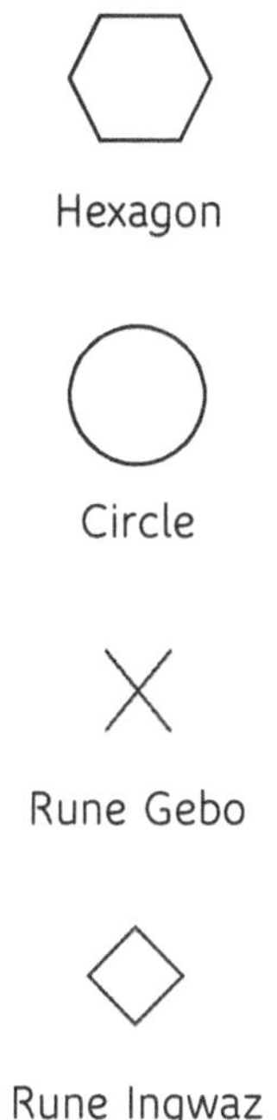

Hexagon

Circle

Rune Gebo

Rune Ingwaz

…and more hidden ones waiting for you to find…

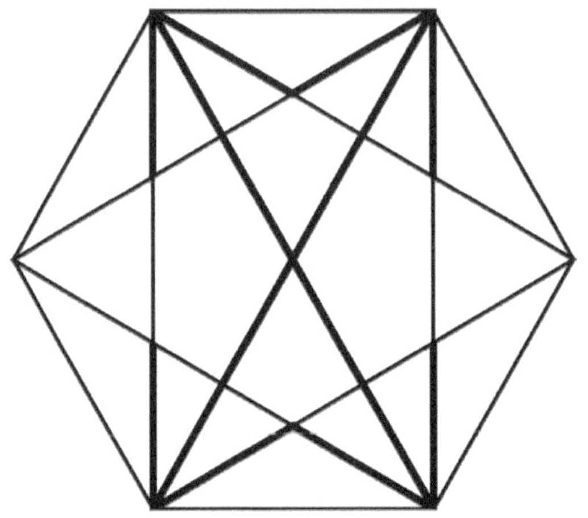

ENERGIZING AND MOTIVATING

This symbol is here to bring us a boost of energy and motivation
whenever we feel energetically down, burned out, or discouraged by
someone or something. Moreover, it bounces away negative
criticism and envy.

SUGGESTED AFFIRMATION

"With this symbol, I ask to be energized and charged with optimism and
motivation."
OR
"I realize that I can't live up to anybody's expectations but my own.
I appreciate all my efforts, as I know they are in tune with my integrity
and spirit."
OR
"I refuse other people's negativity, criticism, and envy,
as only I know what I stand for and why.
I walk my own path, not anybody else's."

SUGGESTED INCANTATION

My willpower is strong.
I walk my path of bliss.
My heart and mind bond
In the light of my spirit.

The symbol consists of the following geometries and runes:

Hexagon

Hexagram

Rune Gebo

Rune Tiwaz

Rune Ingwaz

..and more hidden ones waiting for you to find..

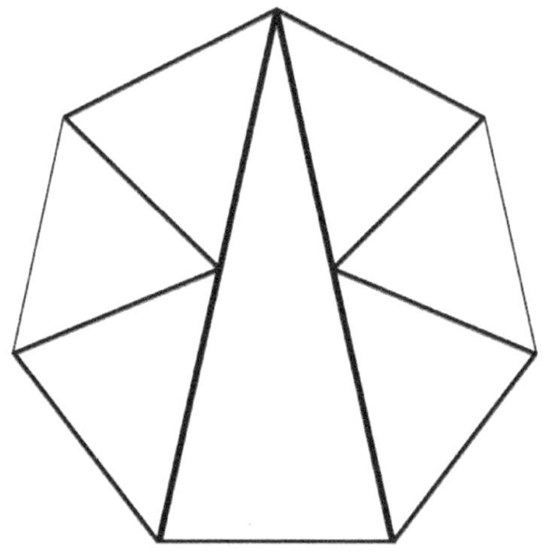

STARTING ANEW

This symbol can give us support when going through significant life
changes that require a fresh start. It brings about courage, motivation,
and strength so that the new cycle may be as harmonious and
favorable as possible.

SUGGESTED AFFIRMATION

"I'm ready to move on from all the situations that no longer serve me
and start again."
OR
"I honor all the past cycles and am willing to learn from them,
but I also welcome new cycles into my life."

SUGGESTED INCANTATION

With this symbol,
I bless this new beginning.
Positive changes are coming.
I accept all the past endings
And welcome new blessings.

The symbol consists of the following geometries and runes:

Septagon

Rune Berkano

Rune Kenaz

..and more hidden ones waiting for you to find.

SUPERCHARGED SYMBOLS FOR METAPHYSICAL PRACTICES

The following supercharged symbols help us boost our psychic

abilities and connect with our divine self and spirit guides.

We were all born with the natural gifts of clairvoyance

(inner seeing), clairsentience (inner sensing),

clairaudience (inner hearing), and others,

but as we grow older we tend to disconnect from them.

The following symbols bind geometries and runes that help us

reconnect with these amazing talents.

DIVINE SELF

This symbol is meant to better our connection with our divine self, the multidimensional, eternal, and innermost part of our spirit. When we fully align with its wisdom, we begin to receive signs and experience synchronicity or sudden spiritual insights and breakthroughs.

SUGGESTED AFFIRMATION

"I honor my divine, eternal self and am open to receiving its guidance and wisdom."

SUGGESTED INCANTATION

I'm a divine being of light.
That is my nature and might.
With its guidance, I thrive.
With its wisdom, I shine.

The symbol consists of the following geometries and runes:

Nine-pointed star (nonagram)

Seven-pointed star (septagram)

Pentagram

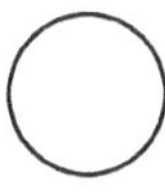

Circle

...and more hidden ones waiting for you to find.

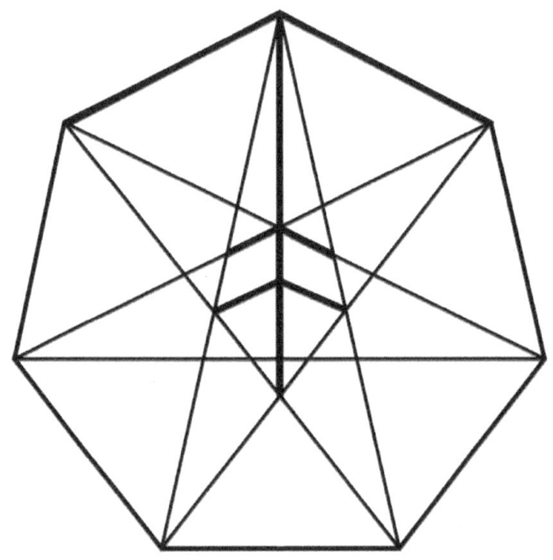

INNER WARRIOR

This symbol helps us unite with our inner warrior, the brave, heroic part of our spirit that is always ready to stand up for ourselves and our loved ones. Working with this symbol naturally brings about the inner warrior virtues: assertiveness, decisiveness, righteousness, determination, confidence, and courage.

SUGGESTED AFFIRMATION

"I honor my inner warrior, the courageous and righteous me who wisely differentiates when it's necessary to be assertive and when to walk away from a fight."
OR
"I ask to receive advice from my inner warrior.
What should I do about this situation?"

SUGGESTED INCANTATION

My inner warrior, the heroic part of me,
Guide me to being righteous and free.
Please, support me throughout my life
So that I'm brave and assertively kind.

The symbol consists of the following geometries and runes:

Septagon

Septagram

Rune Tiwaz

Rune Ansuz

...and more hidden ones waiting for you to find.

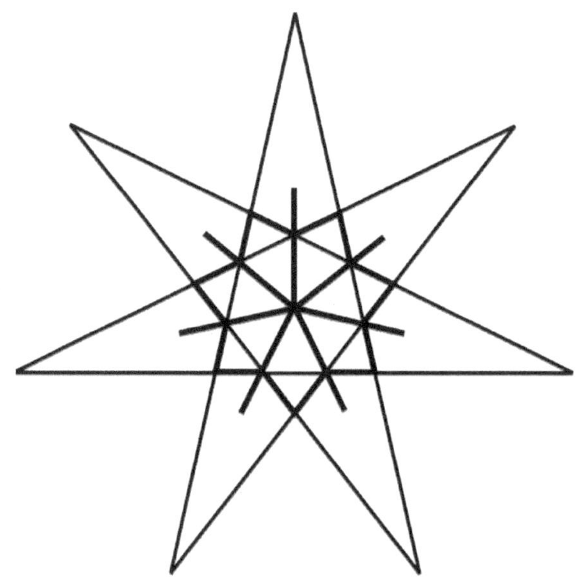

ANGELS AND SPIRIT GUIDES

This symbol was created to help us connect with benevolent beings of light and love. It's best to decide who we wish to communicate with before working with this symbol, whether they are our personal spirit guides, guardian angels, or other types of benevolent deities and ascendant masters who resonate with us.

SUGGESTED AFFIRMATION

"I welcome a clear communication with
(name the spirit guide or deity).
I ask for your advice and guidance regarding (describe the issue)."
OR
"I call upon you now, (name the spirit guide or deity).
Please help me with (describe the issue or situation)."

SUGGESTED INCANTATION

My dear spirit guardians and guides,
Beloved and wise angelic alliance,
I know you're always by my side,
So please bless me with your guidance.

The symbol consists of the following geometries and runes:

Septagram

Seven-pointed star

Rune Algiz

Rune Ehwaz

..and more hidden ones waiting for you to find.

SOUL-FAMILY SPIRIT GUIDES

This symbol was designed to help us contact our soul-family spirit guides and find out more about them. A soul family is a group of souls that likes to incarnate together to evolve. Current family members may or may not be part of our soul family, but you can feel when they are, as these beings are always very dear to us. Our animal friends may also be part of our soul family.

SUGGESTED AFFIRMATION

"I call upon you, my soul-family spirit guides, and ask you to kindly help me with this situation (describe the issue further if you like)."

OR

"I call upon you, my soul-family spirit guides. Please let me understand my spirit's background. Who is part of our soul family and why?"

SUGGESTED INCANTATION

My soul family, my friends,
Help me evolve and grow.
I welcome your guidance.
Please share what you know.

The symbol consists of the following geometries and runes:

Nine-pointed star (nonagram).

Rune Ingwaz

Rune Algiz

Rune Othala

Rune Tiwaz

Rune Ansuz

...and more hidden ones waiting for you to find.

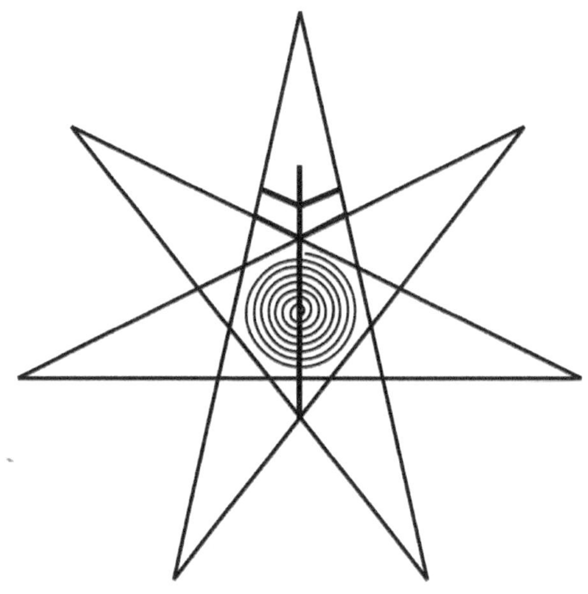

FAIRY FOLK GUIDANCE

This symbol is meant to attune us to the natural world and its multidimensional realms where various fairy folk and nature spirits reside. It may also help us establish a close connection with some of the fairy folk. We should, however, always make sure to call upon benevolent fairy folk, as some tend to dislike humans.

SUGGESTED AFFIRMATION

"I send my love and appreciation to you, benevolent nature spirits and fairy folk who resonate with me and my spirit!
I respect and invite your beautiful presence, wisdom, and guidance."

SUGGESTED INCANTATION

Benevolent spirits of nature, elves, and fairies,
I call upon you who resonate with my spirit.
I now attune to my intuition and sentience
To hear your wisdom and feel your presence.

The symbol consists of the following geometries and runes:

Septagram

Right-turning spiral

Rune Fehu

Rune Algiz

...and more hidden ones waiting for you to find.

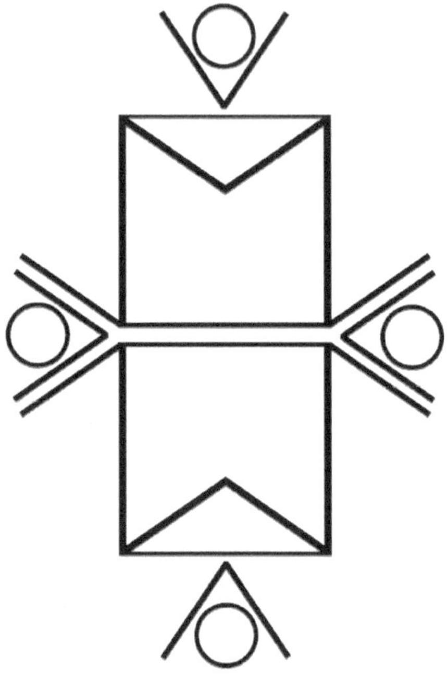

DEEP MEDITATIONS AND JOURNEYS

This symbol blesses metaphysical practices such as deep meditation, channeling, inner journeys, hypnosis, or astral projection. It not only elevates our metaphysical experiences during such practices but also keeps us shielded from negative energies during the whole process.

SUGGESTED AFFIRMATION

"With this symbol, I bless this metaphysical practice
(describe it more if you like)
and ask that it is meaningful, enlightening, and safe."

In my spirit's core,
I seek knowledge and wisdom.
I long to learn more
About that innermost kingdom.

The symbol consists of the following geometries and runes:

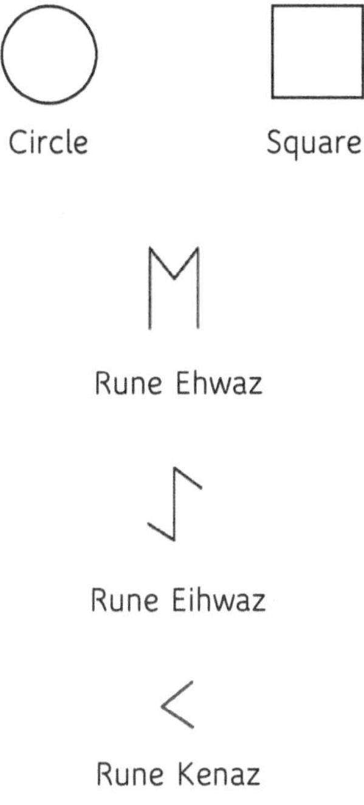

Circle   Square

Rune Ehwaz

Rune Eihwaz

Rune Kenaz

…and more hidden ones waiting for you to find…

SPIRITUAL HOMES

This symbol was designed to help us receive information about those other-dimensional, other planetary, or spiritual homes that our spirit resonates with and likes to return to. It's best to meditate with this symbol before a deep meditation, hypnosis, shamanic journey, astral projection, or other type of metaphysical practice during which we consciously wish to connect with our favorite places in this multiverse.

SUGGESTED AFFIRMATION

"I'm ready to align with my spirit's multidimensional, adventurous self and receive glimpses into my homes in this multiverse."

SUGGESTED INCANTATION

I seek the places my spirit calls home
And that my light body likes to roam.
I ask for glimpses, insights, and information
As I attune to my spirit's favorite locations.

The symbol consists of the following geometries and runes:

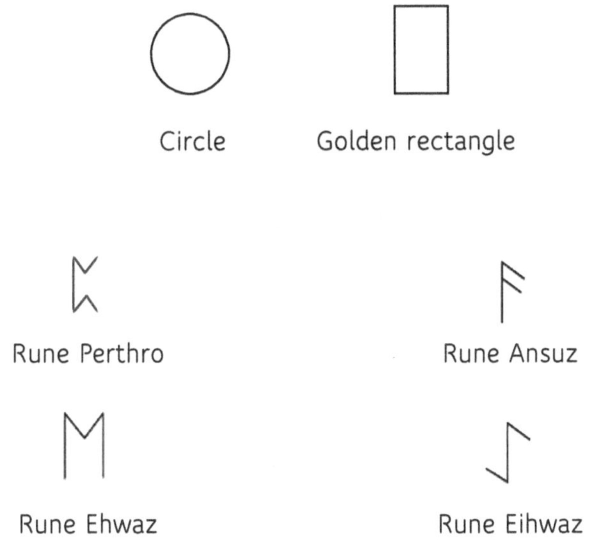

Circle   Golden rectangle

Rune Perthro   Rune Ansuz

Rune Ehwaz   Rune Eihwaz

..and more hidden ones waiting for you to find.

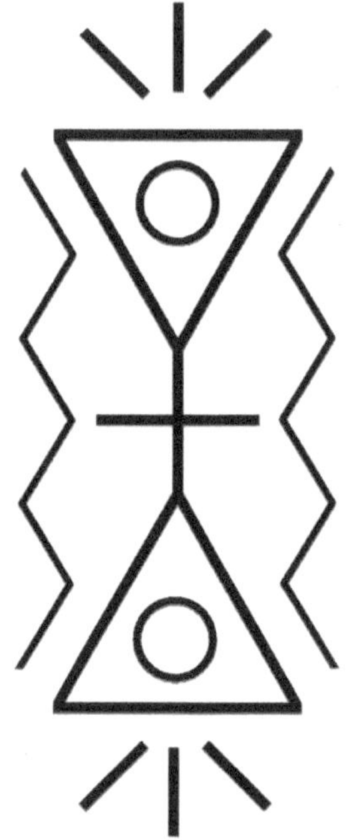

INNER ALCHEMIST

This is the symbol to turn to when we wish to connect with our inner alchemist. It helps us alchemize anything we deem unfavorable into a favorable result. For example, we can alchemize fear into courage, anxiety into calmness, conflict into peace, and so forth.

SUGGESTED AFFIRMATION

"I consciously align with my inner alchemist and ask it to alchemize (name the undesired feeling, emotion, or situation) into (name the desired result)."

As below so above, as above so below,
Aligned with my inner magician I grow.
As within so without, as without so within,
In tune with my inner alchemist, I always win.

The symbol consists of the following geometries and runes:

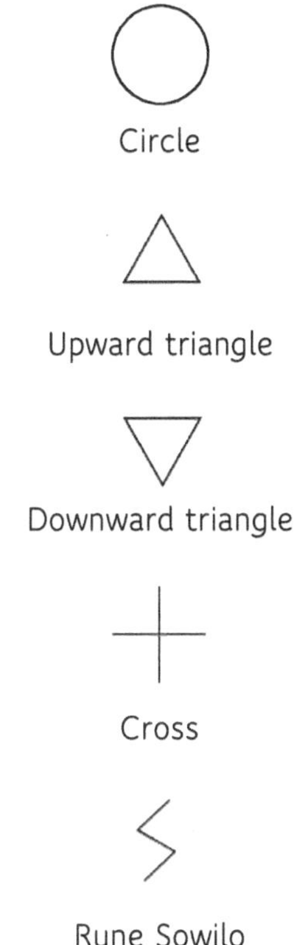

Circle

Upward triangle

Downward triangle

Cross

Rune Sowilo

...and more hidden ones waiting for you to find...

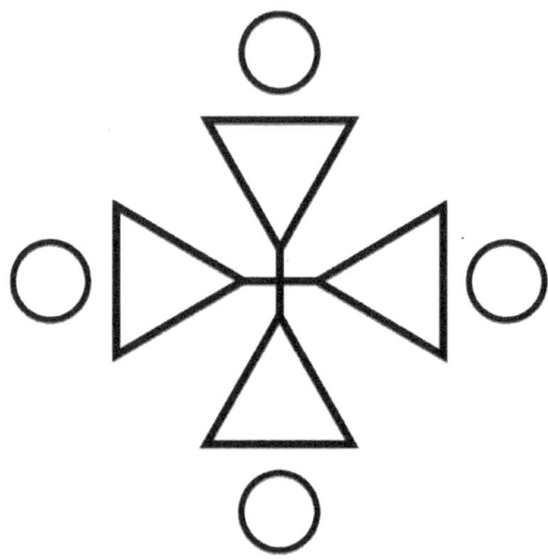

DIVINE INSPIRATION

This symbol is meant to ignite the so-called *awen*, the Old Welsh that translates as "poetic inspiration." During meditations with this symbol, we may receive sudden spiritual insights, knowledge, and wisdom from our own divine, inner library.
It can also help us bless something or someone with a touch of genius – for example, a piece of art or an artist before an important event.

SUGGESTED AFFIRMATION

"In alignment with my divine self, I seek spiritual inspiration and wisdom."
OR
"I'm open to receiving divine, poetic inspiration for (describe the project or occasion)."
OR
"I bless all my future projects and creations with the power of *awen*, the divine inspiration."

For insights and creativity,
I search my inner library.
I seek deep, spiritual wisdom
And welcome divine inspiration!

The symbol consists of the following geometries and runes:

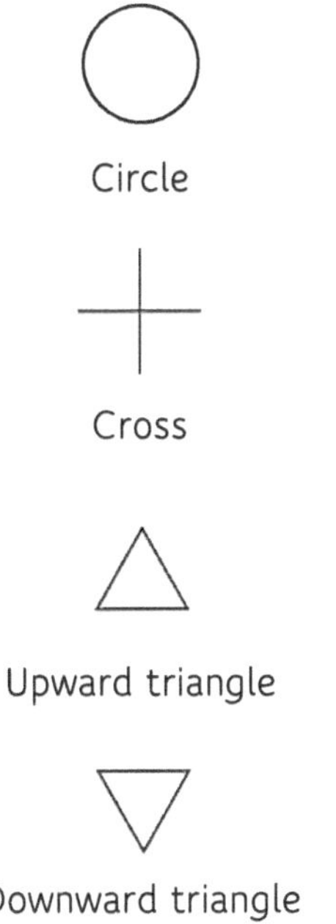

Circle

Cross

Upward triangle

Downward triangle

...and more hidden ones waiting for you to find...

PSYCHIC ABILITIES

This symbol is meant to helps us improve our psychic abilities. It's best to work with it when we are ready to better our clairvoyance (inner seeing), clairaudience (inner hearing), and clairsentience (inner sensing), or to receive any spiritual guidance as clearly and effectively as possible.

SUGGESTED AFFIRMATION

"I align my conscious mind, heart, and soul with my divine self's psychic abilities."
OR
"I aim to work in harmony with my spiritual abilities so that I may evolve and learn more about my divine self and this multiverse."

SUGGESTED INCANTATION

Inner sight,
Inner might,
Inner hearing,
Inner knowing,
I know I have it all within me.

The symbol consists of the following geometries and runes:

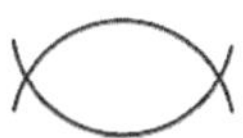

Vesica Piscis

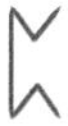

Rune Perthro

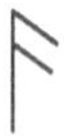

Rune Ansuz

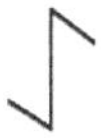

Rune Eihwaz

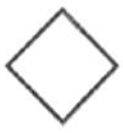

Rune Ingwaz

...and more hidden ones waiting for you to find.

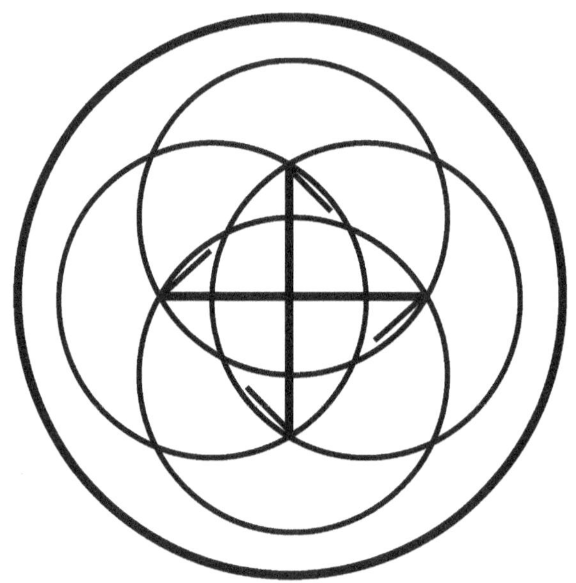

PSYCHIC DREAMS

This symbol helps us receive clear messages from our spirit and divine self before, during, or after sleep. It's best to work with it right before falling asleep with the intention of receiving answers or specific guidance. As a result, we may have meaningful, even psychic, dreams or receive important messages upon awakening. This symbol also improves our memory of dreams.

SUGGESTED AFFIRMATION

"I'm ready to receive answers in my sleep or upon waking regarding this situation (describe the situation)."
OR

"I'm ready for meaningful, insightful dreams tonight.
I'm willing to grasp all the messages and all the advice that my spirit
has for me."
OR
"I'm programing my conscious mind to remember my dreams from now
on. I'm ready to grasp the meanings behind the symbolic language of
my subconscious."

SUGGESTED INCANTATION

I aim for meaningful, wise dreams
As I roam my subconscious streams.
May I receive answers and hints
While asleep or upon waking.

The symbol consists of the following geometries and runes:

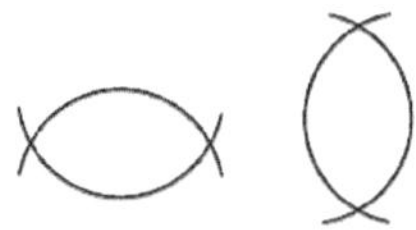

Vesica Piscis/Mandorla

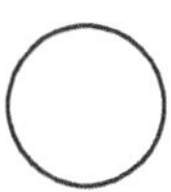

Circle

Rune Eihwaz

..and more hidden ones waiting for you to find.

LIGHT-BODY CONNECTION

This is the symbol of the light body, also known as the spirit body. It was created to help us become more aware of its existence and abilities. It's perfect for people who practice shamanic journeys, astral projection, or inter-dimensional travel, as this symbol may support our light body during such experiences.

SUGGESTED AFFIRMATION

"I want to be conscious of the eternal light body that my spirit uses to roam the realms of the World Tree of Life."
OR
"In alignment with the sovereign power of my divine self, my spirit's light body is safe and roams only benevolent dimensions and timelines."
OR

"I know that my spirit's light body can travel the multiverse and adapt
to various ranges of frequencies but ask to always travel in tune with
life, light, and love."

SUGGESTED INCANTATION

My spirit body, oh, let me feel you!
I know you are part of the real me.
My spirit body, oh, let me sense you!
I know that we are limitless and free.

The symbol consists of the following geometries and runes:

Merkaba

Six-pointed star

Rune Eihwaz

...and more hidden ones waiting for you to find...

SUPERCHARGED SYMBOLS OF THE BASIC ELEMENTS

We are elemental beings who were born to live in harmony with

the five basic elements.

These supercharged symbols are meant to help us embrace our

inner water, air, fire, earth, and ether,

and understand them in a holistic sense.

They may be applied to inner work or magic practices. They can

support the elements in magic circles and other rituals where the

elements play an important role.

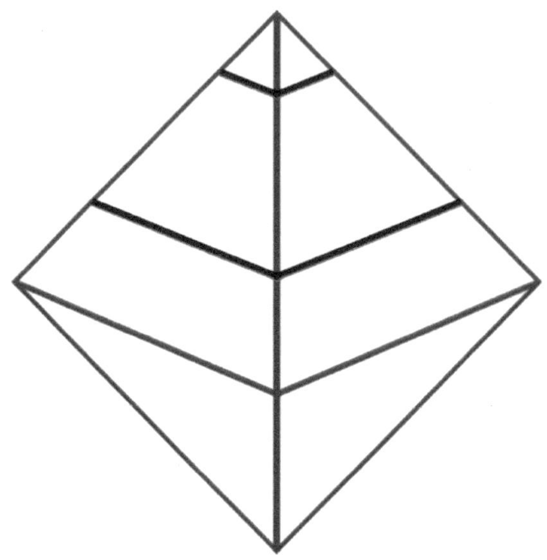

THE AIR ELEMENT

The air element betters our communication skills, helps with the verbalization of ideas, and promotes constructive dialogue. Moreover, it brings light to specific situations and supports positive change. It's best to work with this symbol when we wish to bless the air element, invite its energy into a particular ritual, or strengthen it within our elemental being.

SUGGESTED AFFIRMATION

"I invite the air element into my space now.
Air, help me with (describe the specific situation or magic ritual)."

Blow, wind, blow,
Refresh my mind and soul.
Blow, wind, blow with ease,
I welcome your refreshing breeze.

The symbol consists of the following geometries and runes:

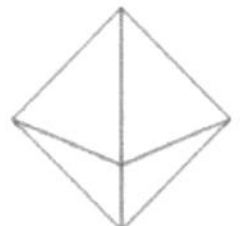

Octahedron

Rune Algiz

Rune Ingwaz

…and more hidden ones waiting for you to find…

THE FIRE ELEMENT

The fire element attracts light, enthusiasm, zeal, and creativity.
Furthermore, it helps with personal empowerment and confidence. It's
best to work with this symbol when we wish to bless the fire element,
invite its energy into a particular ritual, or strengthen it within our
elemental being.

SUGGESTED AFFIRMATION

"I invite the fire element into my space now.
Fire, help me with (describe the situation or magic ritual)."

SUGGESTED INCANTATION

Light up my path, my inner fire,
Fill my life with your light.
Shine through all that I desire,
Support my spirit's might.

The symbol consists of the following geometries and runes:

Circle

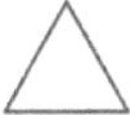

Upward triangle

<

Rune Kenaz

..and more hidden ones waiting for you to find…

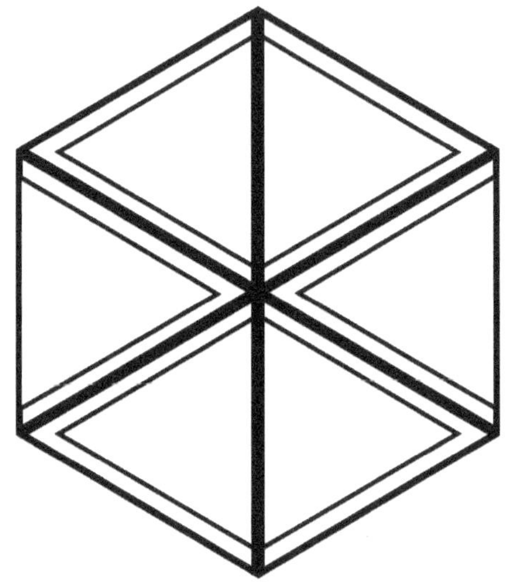

THE EARTH ELEMENT

The earth element supports stability, security, and grounding.
Moreover, it improves our manifestation skills and inspires a greater
connection with nature. It's best to work with this symbol when we
wish to bless the earth element, invite its energy into a particular
ritual, or strengthen it within our elemental being.

SUGGESTED AFFIRMATION

"I invite the earth element into my space now.
Earth, help me with (describe the situation or magic ritual)."

SUGGESTED INCANTATION

Earth is my freedom as well as my base.
Thanks to its existence, I live to create.
In nature's arms, I feel at home and safe.
I welcome its wisdom, guidance, and grace.

The symbol consists of the following geometries and runes:

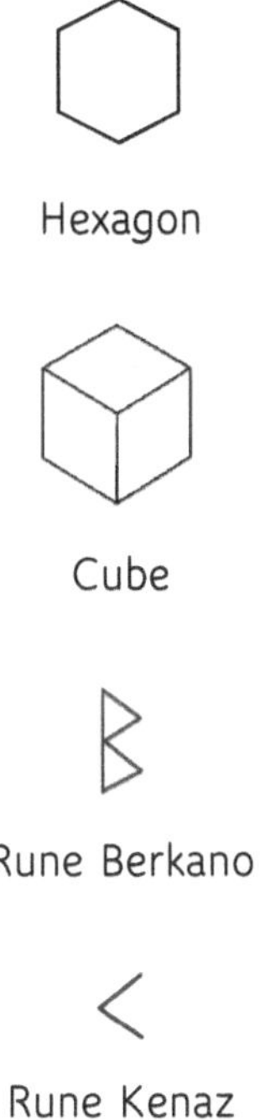

Hexagon

Cube

Rune Berkano

Rune Kenaz

..... and more hidden ones waiting for you to find...

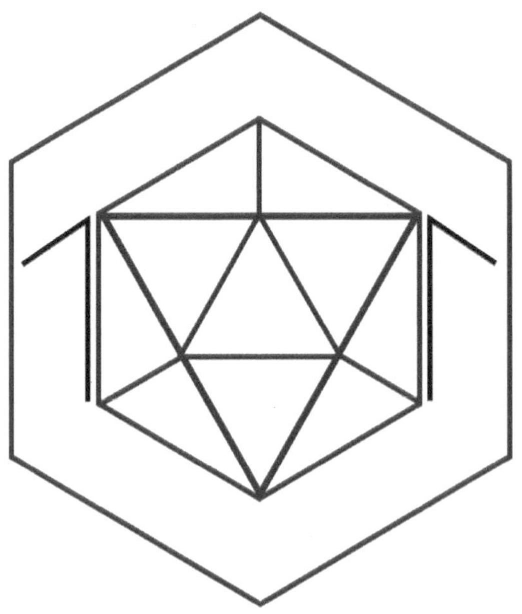

THE WATER ELEMENT

The water element enhances healing, rejuvenation, and revitalization. It also betters our intuition and psychic abilities. It's best to work with this symbol when we wish to bless the water element, invite its energy into a particular ritual, or strengthen it within our elemental being.

SUGGESTED AFFIRMATION

"I invite the water element into my space now.
Water, help me with (describe the situation or magic ritual)."

SUGGESTED INCANTATION

Universal waters above, earthly waters below,
Flow through my body as well as my soul.
Let me move forward and grow,
May I forever be vital and whole.

The symbol consists of the following geometries and runes:

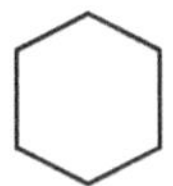

Hexagon

Icosahedron

Rune Laguz

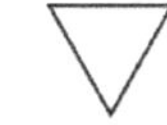

Downward triangle

..... and more hidden ones waiting for you to find...

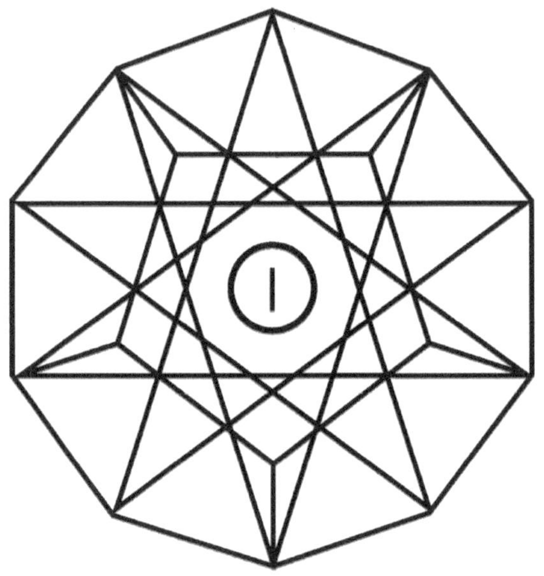

ETHER

The ether is the fifth element that permeates and encompasses all the other elements. It promotes wholeness and unity consciousness, which makes it a powerful ally during meditations, astral travel, divination, spiritism, channeling, and other metaphysical practices. It's best to work with this symbol when we wish to bless the ether, invite its energy into a particular ritual, or strengthen it within our elemental being.

SUGGESTED AFFIRMATION

"I invite the fifth element of the ether into my space now. Ether, help me with (describe the situation or magic ritual)."

SUGGESTED INCANTATION

Ether,
You flow through and around me,
Forever within and without me.
You flow in the living energy field
That heals, connects, and shields.

The symbol consists of the following geometries and runes:

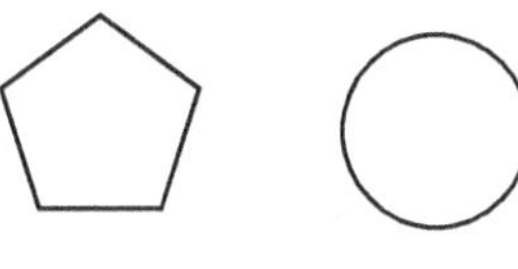

Pentagon   Circle

Dodecahedron

Ten-pointed star/double pentagram

Rune Isa

…... and more hidden ones waiting for you to find…

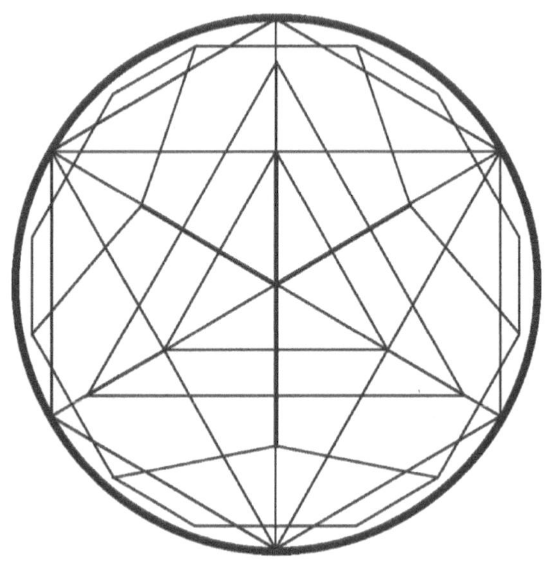

UNITY OF ALL THE BASIC ELEMENTS

This symbol combines the symbolism of the Platonic solids, which represent the basic elements of water, earth, fire, air, and ether. It's best to work with this symbol when we wish to bless these five elements, invite their united energies into a particular ritual, or strengthen them all within our elemental being.

SUGGESTED AFFIRMATION

"I invite all the basic elements into my space now.
I invite the fire element to enlighten me,
the water element to revitalize me,
the earth element to ground me,
the air element to inspire me,
and the ether to complete me.
I unite them all in the divine wholeness.
Powerful, united elements,
help me with (describe the situation or magic ritual)."

Blow, wind, blow,
Flow, water, flow,
Earth, my blessed home,
Fire, the light of my soul,
Ether, my source of healing and wisdom,
I ask you all to unite in my inner kingdom.

The symbol consists of the following geometries and runes:

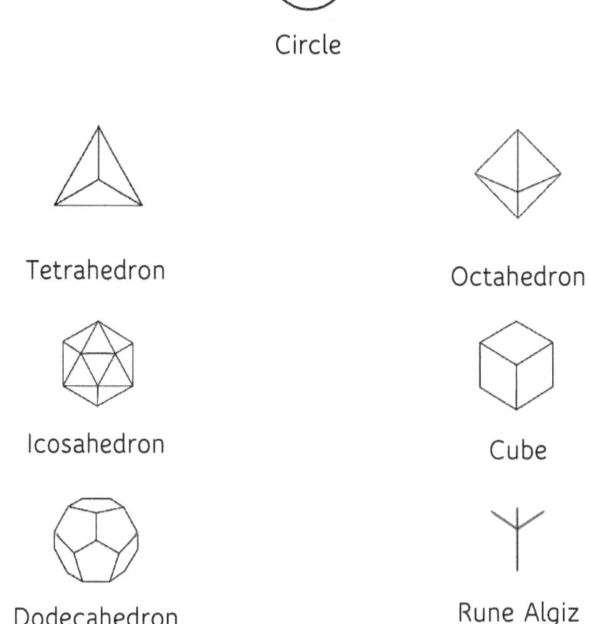

Circle

Tetrahedron

Octahedron

Icosahedron

Cube

Dodecahedron

Rune Algiz

...and more hidden ones waiting for you to find.

SUPERCHARGED ENERGY FIELD SYMBOLS

Each person has their own unique energy field, also known as the electromagnetic field, which is produced by many organs but especially the heart. Many ancient cultures were aware of this and considered the energy field the primary source of our healing, manifesting, and alchemizing abilities. The electromagnetic field is toroidal in shape, and the torus's underlying structure is the so-called vector equilibrium, which is also the geometric pattern used as a base for the following supercharged symbols.

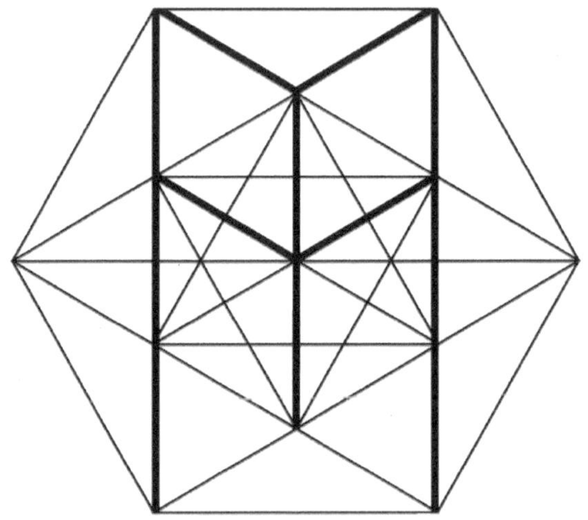

THE ENERGY FIELD'S HEALING QUALITIES

This symbol helps us consciously align with the fantastic self-revitalizing qualities of our energy field and recognize how it works so that we may learn more about our inborn self-healing abilities.

SUGGESTED AFFIRMATION

"I'm ready to achieve a clear connection with my energy field and understand its self-healing mechanisms and processes in order to consciously incorporate them in my life."

SUGGESTED INCANTATION

My energy field is ever flowing,
Innately a part of me.
It's the source of my healing,
Always steady and free.

The symbol consists of the following geometries and runes:"

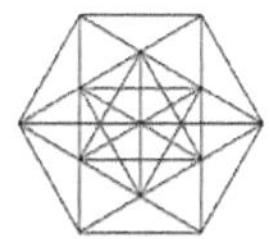

Vector Equilibrium

Rune Uruz

Rune Algiz

Rune Ansuz

Rune Ehwaz

...and more hidden ones waiting for you to find.

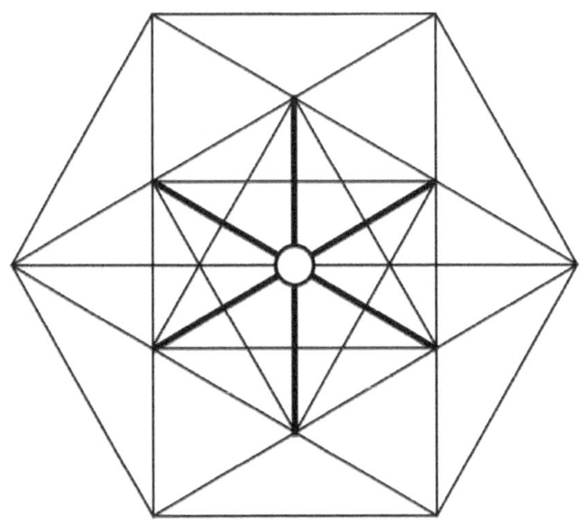

THE ENERGY FIELD'S SHIELDING QUALITIES

This symbol was created to help us understand our energy field's shielding qualities so that it may protect us from negative energies and entities. If other symbols pop up in our mind when we are meditating on it, our subconscious might be unveiling other shielding symbols that we resonate with.

SUGGESTED AFFIRMATION

"I'm ready to achieve a clear connection with my energy field and understand its self-shielding abilities."

Show me, please, my energy field,
Show me my inborn energy shield.
Show me how to stay protected,
Show me how it's all connected.

The symbol consists of the following geometries and runes:

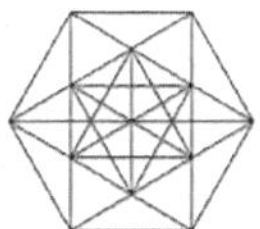

Vector Equilibrium

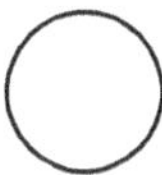

Circle

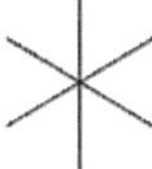

Six-pointed star

...and more hidden ones waiting for you to find

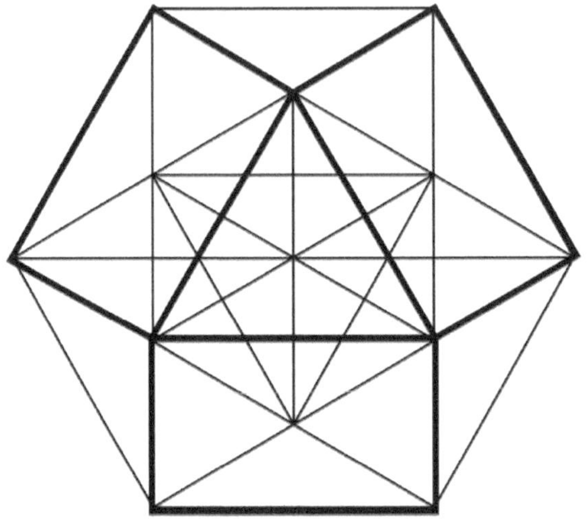

THE ENERGY FIELD'S ALCHEMICAL QUALITIES

This symbol is meant to connect us with our energy field's unique alchemical qualities to learn how to alchemize any negative emotions or tendencies into positive ones. It takes an open mind to work with this symbol, though, as we may also receive telepathic messages about what needs to be alchemized.

SUGGESTED AFFIRMATION

"I'm ready to understand my energy field's alchemical abilities and learn how to work with them in order to live in harmony with myself, others, and the world."

Energy field of mine,
Teach me how to alchemize
All that I dislike into that which I like.

The symbol consists of the following geometries and runes:

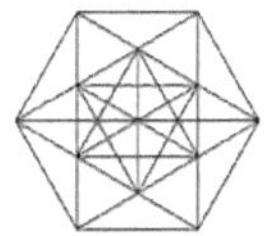

Vector Equilibrium

Golden rectangle

Upward triangle

..and more hidden ones waiting for you to find..

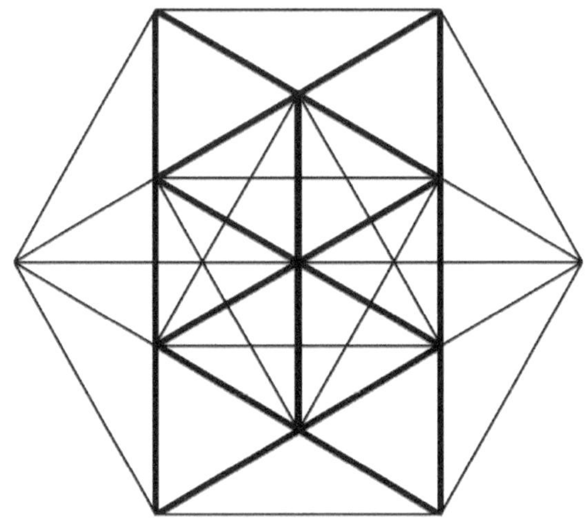

THE ENERGY FIELD'S MANIFESTING ABILITIES

This symbol works magic when we wish to understand the creative and manifesting abilities of our energy field and start working with them. It helps us understand the unique talents of our inner magician and the co-creator we were born to be in this creation.

SUGGESTED AFFIRMATION

"I'm ready to achieve a clear connection with my energy field's manifesting abilities.
I'm ready to start co-creating my life in harmony with the other co-creators around me and to make my dreams come true."

Pure bliss and fulfilment I yield,
In alignment with my energy field.
I am the power, I am the drive,
I live my dreams and dream my life.

The symbol consists of the following geometries and runes:

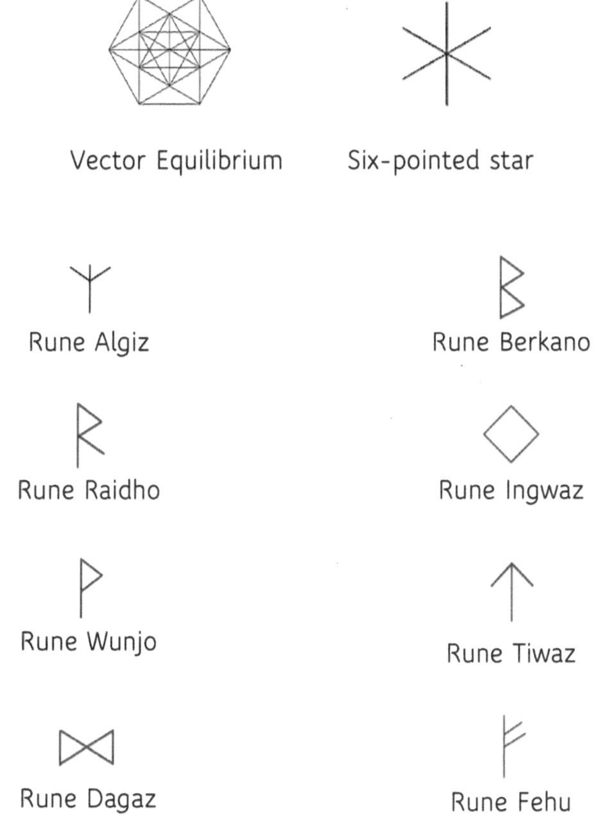

Vector Equilibrium   Six-pointed star

Rune Algiz   Rune Berkano

Rune Raidho   Rune Ingwaz

Rune Wunjo   Rune Tiwaz

Rune Dagaz   Rune Fehu

..and more hidden ones waiting for you to find.

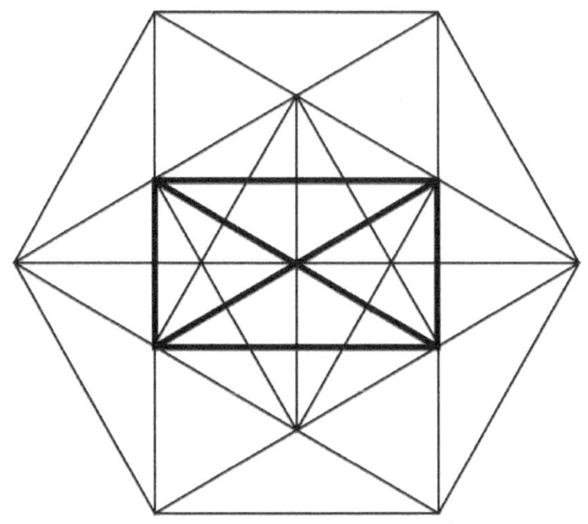

THE ENERGY FIELD'S HARMONY

This symbol helps us recognize the state of our energy field and whether it's in overall harmony. Meditating with it reveals possible weaknesses and shows us how to improve the overall balance in the energy field's flow.

SUGGESTED AFFIRMATION

"I wish to see the state of my energy field. If there are any weaknesses, I program my mind to grasp them now and fix them so that my energy flows freely, steadily, and in overall harmony."

SUGGESTED INCANTATION

Balance me, my energy field,
In your profound energy shield.
Balance me inside out, outward in,
So that I may thrive in harmony.

The symbol consists of the following geometries and runes:

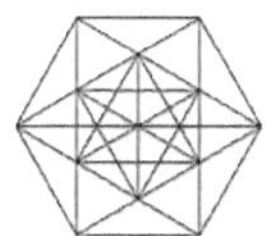

Vector Equilibrium

Golden rectangle

Rune Dagaz

..and more hidden ones waiting for you to find..

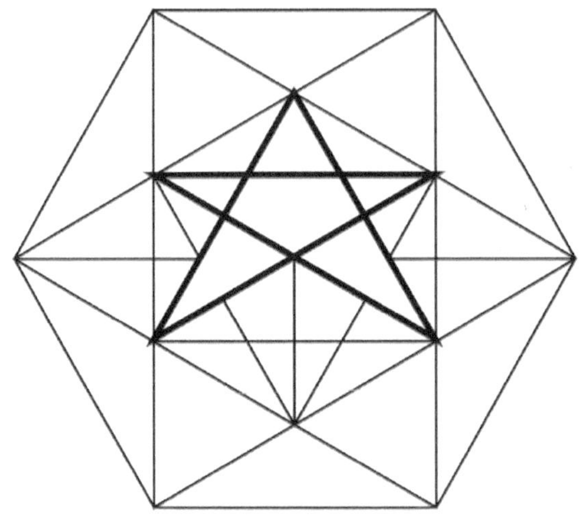

THE ENERGY FIELD'S CONNECTION
TO THE BODY

This symbol was designed to show us what messages or advice our
energy field has for our physical body. It's good to approach this
symbol with an open mind and pay attention to any impressions, ideas,
sensations, or signs to find out whether there's something that could
use improvement.

SUGGESTED AFFIRMATION

"I now consciously connect with my energy field to find out what
messages it has regarding my physical body.
Is there something that I should improve to experience the most vital
and blissful existence in this world?"

SUGGESTED INCANTATION

At one with my energy field I thrive,
Uniting my body, spirit, and mind.
At one with it I am now and forevermore,
Uniting my physical presence and core.

The symbol consists of the following geometries and runes:

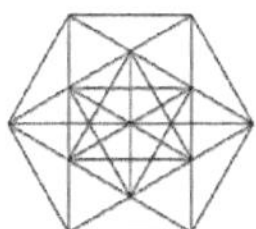

Vector Equilibrium

Pentagram

..and more hidden ones waiting for you to find..

THE ENERGY FIELD'S OVERALL POWER

This symbol helps us consciously align with the immense healing, shielding, and manifesting powers of our energy field and start living in tune with them. While gazing at this image, we may sense how our energy field flows in and out and out and in.

SUGGESTED AFFIRMATION

"I feel my energy field and its profound healing, shielding, and manifesting powers.
I'm now ready to embrace them and start living them."

SUGGESTED INCANTATION

Energy field, let me feel my source,
My divine self, light body, and soul.
Embrace me in your profound force,
Make me vital, peaceful, and whole.

The symbol consists of the following geometries and runes:

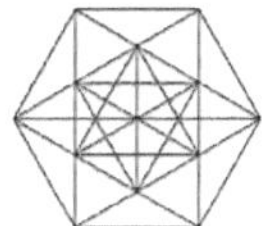

Vector Equilibrium

Seed of Life

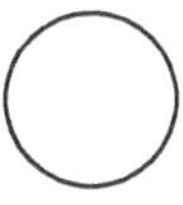

Circle

..and more hidden ones waiting for you to find...

SUPERCHARGED MEDITATION SYMBOLS

The following supercharged symbols are based on the coalescence of circles of the same circumference, which results in some of the most profound sacred geometry symbols like the vesica piscis, the Seed of Life, and the Flower of Life. Since some of these symbols would be difficult to draw by hand, they are meant for meditation. The magic happens simply by gazing at them. Like the other supercharged symbols in this book, the following ones also bind powerful runes, which enhances their overall purpose.

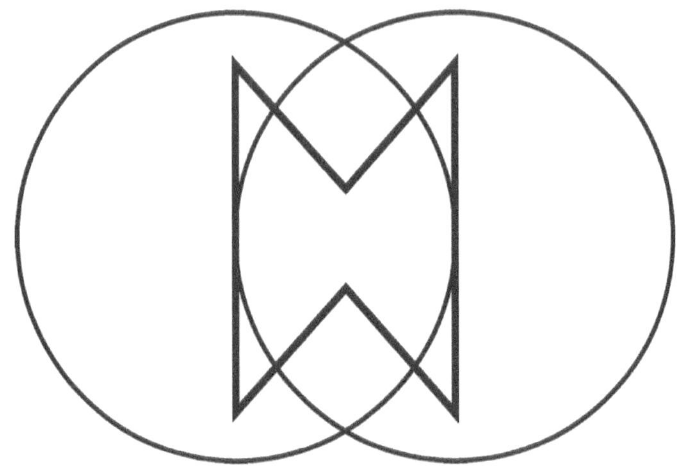

AKASHIC RECORDS

This symbol is meant to help us tune in to the memory of the
multiverse, the so-called Akashic records. In Norse mythology, these
records are guarded by timekeepers called Norns, giantesses who spin
the threads of destiny. With the help of this symbol, we may receive
specific information, inspiration, knowledge, or wisdom from the
universal field of consciousness.

SUGGESTED AFFIRMATION

"I'm ready to connect with the memory of the multiverse.
My mind is open to receiving guidance and advice now."

SUGGESTED INCANTATION

Memory of the multiverse,
Show me how to immerse
In your profound wisdom
To obtain insight and vision.

The symbol consists of the following geometries and runes:

Vesica Piscis

Rune Perthro

Rune Ehwaz

..and more hidden ones waiting for you to find.

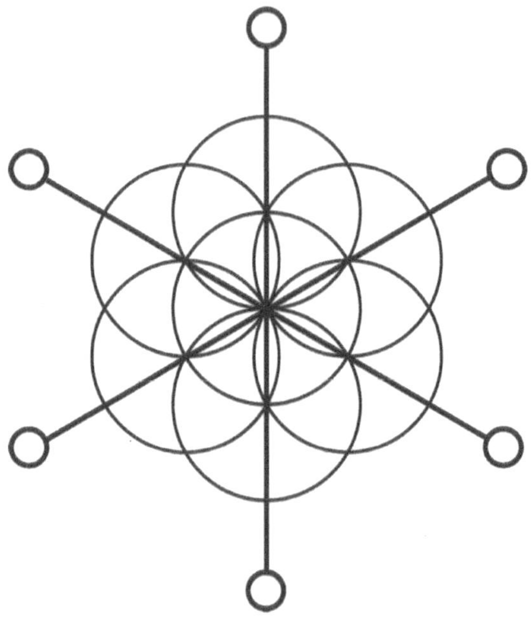

ALL WITHIN ONE AND ONE WITHIN ALL

This symbol was designed to help us achieve a deep meditative state in which we can focus on the interconnectedness between ourselves and the multiverse.

SUGGESTED AFFIRMATION

"I wish to experience the all within me and me within the all."

Oneness, unity
Within me, around me.
Wholeness, divinity
Around me, within me.

The symbol consists of the following geometries and runes:

Six-pointed star

Seed of Life

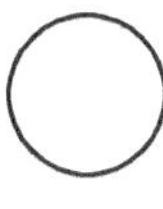

Circle

…and more hidden ones waiting for you to find…

SHADOW AND LIGHT

This symbol can assist us in recognizing our shadow, finding its meaning, and balancing it with our light. Moreover, it inspires us to look at the light and dark aspects of others and the world, which is especially useful when we want to find a reason behind a particular injustice.

SUGGESTED AFFIRMATION

"I recognize my shadow and instead of letting it control me, I let it support my light."
OR
"I'm ready to see the true meaning of light and darkness in me, in others, and in the world."

A little shadow saves me from burning
Just as light saves me from withering.
I respite in shadow but live from light.
No outside forces can affect my might.

The symbol consists of the following geometries and runes:

Flower of Life

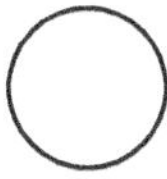

Circle

Rune Kenaz

Rune Dagaz

…. and more hidden ones waiting for you to find…

RELATIONSHIP CONNECTIONS

This symbol helps us find out why we are drawn to a specific person or why we are attracted to certain types of personalities. Moreover, it may unveil the hidden interconnections between people, places, and situations. While meditating with this symbol, it's essential to pay attention to sudden insights or impressions.

SUGGESTED AFFIRMATION

"I'm ready to understand why I'm attracted to this person or this type of personality."
OR

"I wish to uncover the deeper connection between me and (the person's name)."
OR
"I want to understand the hidden meaning behind this (describe the relationship or situation you wish to understand better)."

SUGGESTED INCANTATION

I seek meaning behind what's repeating,
I know that what we have planted we are reaping.

The symbol consists of the following geometries and runes:

Flower of Life

Rune Mannaz

Rune Wunjo

Rune Algiz

… and more hidden ones waiting for you to find…

REVIVAL

This symbol has been charged with the power of revival. It can calm
and refresh us after a distressing experience. Moreover, it helps us
better understand events that have taken place or the past cycles that
have ended so that we may learn from them and start anew.

SUGGESTED AFFIRMATION

"I'm ready to heal and revive my body, mind, heart, and soul so that I
can go on living my life in contentment and joy."
OR
"I'm ready to fully accept what has transpired and understand why it
has happened so that I can move on from this situation."

SUGGESTED INCANTATION

Peace and wholeness I feel,
As the wheels of change spin.
Peace and wholeness I feel,
In the power of what's within.

The symbol consists of the following geometries and runes:

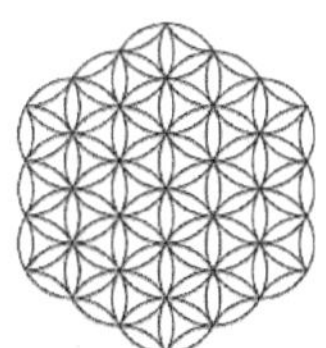

Flower of Life

Rune Berkano

Rune Gebo

Rune Wunjo

Rune Algiz

... and more hidden ones waiting for you to find...

SOOTHING MEDITATION

This symbol has a soothing, calming effect and is meant to bring about
a relaxed state of mind. It's helpful to gaze at it whenever we feel
stressed, worried, or anxious. While meditating with it, it's good to
focus our attention on that eternal, divine part of our spirit where we
find peace and wholeness.

SUGGESTED AFFIRMATION

"With this symbol, I bring my attention to that innermost, eternal, and
divine part of my spirit where I find comfort, peace, and wholeness."

SUGGESTED INCANTATION

My mind is ready to calm down,
Peace moves around and around.
Spins me in that wholesome state of mind
That my divine self perpetually provides.

The symbol consists of the following geometries and runes:

Flower of Life

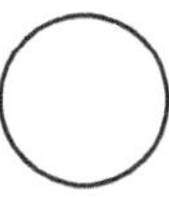

Circle

Six-pointed star

…. and more hidden ones waiting for you to find…

POSITIVITY AND GRATITUDE

This symbol has the power to lift our spirits when we're feeling down. It helps boost our mood and allows us to achieve a positive outlook on things. It also brings about happiness and gratitude and encourages us to focus on what we do have instead of what we don't. It's best to meditate with this symbol in an outdoor environment such as a garden or by a tree because nature boosts its effect.

SUGGESTED AFFIRMATION

"I'm grateful for (describe all that you feel grateful for at the moment)."
OR

"My divine self, the eternal part of my spirit, please guide me and help
me focus on the positive aspects of my life and this world.
Deep inside, I feel the willingness and excitement to live and learn."

SUGGESTED INCANTATION

Just as nature bustles with joy and life,
So I wish to be happy and thrive!

The symbol consists of the following geometries and runes:

Flower of Life

Rune Wunjo

Rune Algiz

Rune Tiwaz

... and more hidden ones waiting for you to find...

SPIRIT ANIMAL, ANIMAL GUIDES &
COMPANIONS

This is a symbol to turn to when we wish to establish or improve
telepathic communication with our spirit animals and animal guides, or
our animal companions who are often their earthly incarnations.
Meditating with it helps us connect with them, so it's good to pay
attention to any sudden insights or thoughts, as these may hold
important messages.

SUGGESTED AFFIRMATION

"I'm ready to connect with my spirit animals.
I'm open to their wisdom and guidance."
OR

"I'm ready to telepathically communicate with my animal companion
(say the animal's name and specify whether it's a current or late
animal friend)."
OR
"Please, my beloved animal spirit guides, provide me with help and
support in this situation (describe it)."

SUGGESTED INCANTATION

My spirit animals, my animal guides,
Bless me with your wisdom and advice.
I wish to imbibe and fully enjoy
Your kindness, innocence, and joy.
My dearest animal companions,
I honor our love, bond, and union.

The symbol consists of the following geometries and runes:

Flower of Life

Rune Uruz

Rune Wunjo

Rune Fehu

Rune Ansuz

... and more hidden ones waiting for you to find..

ANSWERS

This symbol helps us receive answers to any questions we may have.
Therefore, it's crucial to pay attention to the thoughts or impressions
that permeate our mind while meditating on this symbol, as they should
contain the information and guidance we seek.

SUGGESTED AFFIRMATION

"I'm willing to receive the answer to the following question:
(describe it)."

Truthful answers I seek
In situations like these.
May I feel, may I discern,
What I'm supposed to learn.

The symbol consists of the following geometries and runes:

Flower of Life

Rune Ingwaz

...and more hidden ones waiting for you to find...

MULTIDIMENSIONALITY

This symbol helps us connect with our multidimensionality and the selves that co-exist in different planes of existence or different timelines. While meditating on this symbol, we can even receive glimpses into our currently relevant past, future, or interdimensional incarnations.

SUGGESTED AFFIRMATION

"If it resonates with my current here and now, I'm open to receiving guidance and messages from my other incarnations, whether they are on a different timeline or in another dimension."

SUGGESTED INCANTATION

Aligned with my divine self,
I'm ready to wisely experience
My multidimensional variants
And who I was, am, and will be next.

The symbol consists of the following geometries and runes:

Flower of Life

Rune Algiz

Rune Eihwaz

Rune Ehwaz

…. and more hidden ones waiting for you to find…

ORIGINS, CURRENT PURPOSE, AND AIMS

This symbol can be of great assistance when we wish to receive answers about where our spirit came from, why it's here, and where it's heading next. Meditating on it may bring spontaneous realizations and might also attract further guidance via signs and synchronicity.

SUGGESTED AFFIRMATION

"I'm ready to know where my spirit came from, why it's here, and where it's heading after this incarnation."
OR
"I'm open to receiving answers regarding
my spirit's origins, current purpose, and future goals."

SUGGESTED INCANTATION

In my spirit's home I thrive,
In my spirit's truth I abide.
I'm ready to see my past, current, and future aims,
And the overall purpose behind these earthly games.

The symbol consists of the following geometries and runes:

Flower of Life

Rune Othala

Rune Raidho

Rune Ansuz

…and more hidden ones waiting for you to find…

INNER MOON

This symbol helps us connect with our inner moon, the source of our inborn intuition, sensitivity, and psychic abilities. Meditating with it tends to soothe us, so it's beneficial during any kind of emotional turmoil or when we simply need to relax. Moreover, it can prepare us for metaphysical work such as meditation, astral projection, hypnosis, spiritism, channeling, and so forth.

SUGGESTED AFFIRMATION

"I connect with my inner moon and let it nourish my intuition, sensitivity, and psychic abilities."

SUGGESTED INCANTATION

My moon, show me the way
To that safe, innermost cave.
In its darkness I perceive the light
Of my innermost hearing and sight.

The symbol consists of the following geometries and runes:

Flower of Life

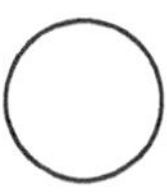

Circle

Rune Mannaz

Rune Dagaz

Rune Kenaz

…. and more hidden ones waiting for you to find…

INNER SUN

This symbol helps us connect with our inner sun, the source of our personal willpower, self-appreciation, and self-esteem. Meditating with it may boost our energy levels and fill us with optimism. It can also help empower us before important decisions or meetings.

SUGGESTED AFFIRMATION

"I connect with my inner sun and let it rouse my inner strength, confidence, and optimism."

SUGGESTED INCANTATION

My sun, please shine on me and through me,
May I always glow with optimism and glee.
I know I have the power to choose for myself
If I embrace my divine power and confidence.

The symbol consists of the following geometries and runes:

Flower of Life

Rune Dagaz

Rune Sowilo

Rune Kenaz

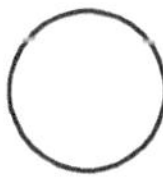

Circle

…. and more hidden ones waiting for you to find…

SYNCHRONICITY

This symbol can be very useful when we have witnessed interesting synchronicity and want to know why. Meditating with it may help us understand what these recurring signs are guiding us to.

SUGGESTED AFFIRMATION

"I'm ready to understand why I keep experiencing this synchronicity (describe it in more detail if you like)."

SUGGESTED INCANTATION

I'm open to receiving messages and signs
From my divine self and my spirit guides.
Synchronicity, what are you telling me?
Synchronicity, what does this all mean?

The symbol consists of the following geometries and runes:

Flower of Life

Rune Ehwaz

Rune Laguz

... and more hidden ones waiting for you to find...

KEEP THE MAGIC GOING!

9 7 8 8 0 1 1 0 0 5 4 3 6